capturing the wisdom of practice

professional portfolios for educators

giselle o. martin-kniep

ASCD Association for Supervision and Curriculum Development • Alexandria, Virginia USA

Association for Supervision and Curriculum Development
1703 N. Beauregard St. • Alexandria, VA 22311-1714 USA
Telephone: 1-800-933-2723 or 703-578-9600 • Fax: 703-575-5400
Web site: http://www.ascd.org • E-mail: member@ascd.org

Gene R. Carter, *Executive Director*
Michelle Terry, *Associate Executive Director, Program Development*
Nancy Modrak, *Director, Publishing*
John O'Neil, *Director of Acquisitions*
Mark Goldberg, *Development Editor*
Julie Houtz, *Managing Editor of Books*
Jo Ann Irick Jones, *Senior Associate Editor*
Charles D. Halverson, *Project Assistant*
Gary Bloom, *Director, Design and Production Services*
Georgia McDonald, *Senior Designer*
Tracey A. Smith, *Production Manager*
Dina Murray, *Production Coordinator*
John Franklin, *Production Coordinator*
Nedalina Dineva/M. L. Coughlin Editorial Services, *Indexer*
Barton Matheson Willse & Worthington, *Desktop Publisher*

Printed in the United States of America.

s10/99

ASCD Stock No.: 199254
ASCD member price: $16.95 nonmember price: $20.95

Library of Congress Cataloging-in-Publication Data

Martin-Kniep, Giselle O.
Capturing the wisdom of practice : professional portfolios for educators / Giselle O. Martin-Kniep.
p. cm.
Includes bibliographical references and index.
"ASCD stock no.: 199254"
ISBN 0-87120-345-6
1. Teachers—Rating of—United States. 2. School administrators—Rating of—United States. 3. Portfolios in education—United States. I. Title.
LB1728 .M27 1999
371.14'4—dc21 99-6646
CIP

04 03 02 01 00 99 10 9 8 7 6 5 4 3 2 1

CAPTURING THE WISDOM OF PRACTICE: PROFESSIONAL PORTFOLIOS FOR EDUCATORS

List of Figures iv

Acknowledgments v

Introduction 1

Chapter 1
What Are Professional Portfolios? 3

Chapter 2
Portfolios for Teachers 13

Chapter 3
Portfolios for School Administrators 17

Chapters 4
Teacher/Administrator-as-Learner Portfolios 27

Chapter 5
Teacher-as-Curriculum-and-Assessment-Developer Portfolios 42

Chapter 6
The Role of Inquiry in Professional Portfolios 67

Chapter 7
Practical Strategies for Getting Started 80

Appendixes

1: Hudson Valley Portfolio Assessment Project Checklist for the Review of Teacher-as-Assessor Portfolio 85
2: Hendrick Hudson School District Portfolio Initiative Guidelines 87
3: Hendrick Hudson Teacher/Administrator-as-Learner Portfolio Rubric 91
4: Hilton School District CLASSIC Initiative Rubric 95
5: Teacher/Administrator-as-Learner Portfolio Rubric 101
6: Teacher-as-Curriculum-and-Assessment-Developer Portfolio Rubric 103
7: Teacher/Administrator-as-Researcher Portfolio Rubric 108
8: Teacher/Administrator-as-Professional-Developer Portfolio Rubric 110

Bibliography and Recommended Resources 112

Index 115

About the Author 119

FIGURES

1.1. Excerpt from CLASSIC Rubric's Goal #2: Emphasis on Reflective Thinking 11
3.1. A Superintendent's Organizational Map Illustrates His Vision for the District 21
4.1. Teacher/Administrator-as-Learner Rubric for an Exemplary Portfolio 29
4.2. Students' Personal Goals Planning Sheet 31
4.3. Students' Reflection Form 32
4.4. 3rd Grader Kelly Explains Her Choice of a Portfolio Selection 33
4.5. 3rd Grader Alicia Explains Her Choice of a Portfolio Selection 34
4.6. A Teacher's Pre- and Post-Concept Map of Her Understanding of Assessment 40
5.1. Teacher-as-Curriculum-and-Assessment-Developer Rubric for an Exemplary Portfolio 44
5.2. Excerpt from a 2nd Grade Language Arts Curriculum Map 47
5.3. Problem-Solving Rubric for a 4th Grade Mathematics Class 49
5.4. A Project Web Developed by a 6th Grade Class 50
5.5. Guidelines for 6th Graders in Selecting Portfolio Entries 51
5.6. Questions to Guide 6th Graders' Reflections on Their Portfolio Selections 52
5.7. Rating Sheet for Book Projects in 6th Grade Language Arts 55
5.8. Rubric for Book Projects in 6th Grade Language Arts 56
5.9. Rubric for Journey Through the Western Hemisphere Project 57
5.10. Reflective Questions for Journey Through the Western Hemisphere Project 58
5.11. Rubric for the Newspaper Find-a-Job Project 59
5.12. Student- and Teacher-Designed Rubric for a 7th Grade Presentation Project 60
5.13. A 7th Grader's Outline for a Presentation Project 61
5.14. Excerpts from 2nd Grader Jeanne's Weekly Log and Her Teacher's Responses 63
6.1. Teacher/Administrator-as-Researcher Rubric for an Exemplary Portfolio 68
6.2. Teacher/Administrator-as-Professional-Developer Rubric for an Exemplary Portfolio 69
6.3. 7th Graders' *General* Reflections on Question #1: How Do You Feel About Our Process for Writing a Descriptive Essay? 71
6.4. 7th Graders' *Specific* Reflections on Question #2: What Areas of Spelling Do You Find Difficult? 72
6.5. A Comparison of Traditional and Authentic Tasks 77

Acknowledgments

I could not have written this book without the inspiration provided by the teachers and administrators who developed the portfolios on which this book is based. I have attempted to honor the legacy of such learning by including and acknowledging their work so as to make it accessible to others. I wish I could have captured the voices of all of them, but space did not allow that. I thank all of them for their trust and their commitment.

I thank Diane Cunningham, my friend and associate, for her thoughtful reading of portfolios and my work, and for helping me articulate what I know and what I am struggling to understand. I also thank Mark Goldberg, ASCD development editor, for making this book a journey worth embracing and for facilitating its writing.

There are others whom I owe so much:

Nanette, for teaching me about integrity.
Carl, for showing me what is possible.
Leah, for letting me in.

—Giselle O. Martin-Kniep

Introduction

Exhilarating, frustrating, predictable. Teaching can be all of these things and more. At best, it is an elegant dialogue in which the teacher creates possibilities that the learner finds compelling. At worse, it is a calculated ritual where much is said but nothing is heard. Even the best teachers cannot do the former all the time, because good teaching, to some extent, depends on the learner as well. We cannot force learners to learn, only invite them.

Teaching is an act of inspiration. Whereas effective teachers, like good actors, draw such inspiration from within, they need the audience's response to produce desired effects. As in acting, the teacher's performance can be based on a script that can be enacted repeatedly, but, unlike in acting, the script has to be amended, even discarded, if the audience cannot understand it. There is no such thing as the perfect lesson. Plays will be considered brilliant even if a given audience does not like them. Lessons are partial failures when a single student cannot learn from them. Teaching is an interactive art that can never be understood independently from its effects. It is a highly complex combination of specialized knowledge, skills, and dispositions. Herein lies the problem of capturing teachers' expertise.

Most of us remember a few teachers who, for good or bad, shaped our lives. Those of us who studied in schools of education remember that most of our professors weren't practicing teachers in schools. They had studied teaching and, perhaps, taught in schools at some point in their lives. Yet their credentials and legitimacy were based on what they knew *about* teaching rather than in what they could do in the very settings where they taught us to function. Even when our professors and instructors were models of good teaching, the programs in which we learned about teaching were, for the most part, divorced from the contexts that would have allowed us to put our learning about teaching and learning to a test.

Thus, as students of teaching, we had to leave the setting that gave us the license to teach, often without truly learning about the profession of teaching. Once in schools, as we became inducted into the profession, we realized how little we knew and how much more we needed to learn. Paradoxically, despite the process of moving from beginners to skilled professionals with apparent access to continuous education through inservice experiences, we also realized how the education culture gives lip service to the meaning of "professional."

Physicians teach, monitor, and produce the knowledge base that informs their professional activities, as do accountants and lawyers. Teachers typically don't teach, monitor, or produce the knowledge base of other teachers. That's where professional portfolios come in. Through portfolios teachers document the essence of their work and thus create an environment in which teachers can legitimately produce, teach, and monitor the profession.

During the past five years, I have learned about and used professional portfolios in much of my work as an educational researcher and consultant. My experiences as a student of educational change have taught me that fostering teacher and school change is a tremendously complex endeavor that defies much of what we do in the name of school restructuring and teacher education. I have been extremely fortunate to be able to design and implement a number of different initiatives with teachers over several years. Much of this work was aimed at helping teachers develop and use alternative forms of student assessment and integrated curriculum units. To date, this work has resulted in over 30 school-based and regional efforts comprising over 3,000 teachers and 100 administrators from over 400 school districts. In all of these initiatives, teachers have developed portfolios to compile, reflect upon, and receive feedback on ongoing drafts of curriculum and assessment work.

As a professional developer and continuing learner of my craft, I have come to understand much about these portfolios. In fact, they have become the primary means by which I have learned about teaching and learning. Over time, my thinking about portfolios has evolved, enabling me to test different structures and to experiment with different roles for myself and for the teachers with whom I have worked.

Professional portfolios have been endorsed by the National Board for Professional Teaching Standards, by the state of Texas, and by numerous school districts in an effort to acknowledge and certify teacher expertise. However, portfolios are the exception rather than the rule as either tools for self-assessment or as mechanisms for teacher evaluation and supervision. Just as students need explicit criteria and models of refection, teachers need access to similar criteria and exemplars.

Administrators are also developing professional portfolios, for example, when searching for a new position and legitimizing their expertise. Moreover, some districts, such as Canandaigua School District and Manhasset School District, both in New York, require such portfolios in their recruitment and hiring practices.

In this book, we will take a close look at professional portfolios. Although my experience has been mostly with teachers, I've also worked with administrators in developing portfolios. Because my efforts have been primarily with teachers, most of the examples in the book (except for those in Chapter 3) come from teachers' portfolios. Much of the general information about portfolios, however, applies to administrators as well.

In Chapter 1, I will discuss what portfolios are, the contexts in which they are used, and how they are structured. We'll also look at a three-part simulation process I use to start teachers and administrators thinking about portfolios and, then, my specific experiences working with educators and portfolios. In Chapter 2, we'll examine portfolios for teachers; in Chapter 3, portfolios for school administrators. In Chapters 4 through 6, I will focus on four types of portfolios: teacher/administrator-as-learner, teacher-as-curriculum-and-assessment-developer, teacher/administrator-as-researcher, and teacher/administrator-as-professional-developer. Chapter 7 contains starting points and practical strategies for developing and using portfolios.

1 What Are Professional Portfolios?

A portfolio not only forces you to think deeply, which is a good thing in and of itself; it then stores those thoughts for later use.

—Tim Sergeant, middle school teacher
Canandaigua Middle School
Canandaigua, New York

Portfolios enable educators to improve upon, portray, and assess their work. They are collections of purposeful and specialized work, capturing a process that can never be fully appreciated unless one can be inside and outside someone else's mind. They validate current expectations and legitimize future goals.

Portfolios are history in the making. They are fluid, even though they can freeze a moment and make it look as if it has a clear beginning and end. They are museums of our work and thinking—displaying our successes, experiments, and dreams. Portfolios are mirrors, albeit distorted, of an evolving reality. They tell us what we want to see and what we wish we would not see. In addition to a looking glass into the self, portfolios are a professional looking glass. Here's how one teacher expressed it:

> After looking at my portfolio, I realize how important self-reflection is to my personal and professional growth. Reflective thinking and writing force me to ask myself essential questions about what and how I teach. I am once again the learner—a rewarding role.
>
> *—Jeanne Robillard, 4th grade teacher*
> *Ontario Elementary School, Ontario, New York*

Portfolios are also substantive documents. In teaching, substance is produced by presenting events in context. For example, a performance assessment involving a student debate on the merits and shortcomings of certain school regulations is best understood if we know certain contextual information, such as the lessons that preceded the assessment, the outcomes the teacher sought to address, the time and resources required for students to acquire desired knowledge and skills, and the success of the assessment with different students. In other words, assessment, curriculum, and instruction cannot be judged independently from one another when we are trying to understand their value and consequences.

Contexts for Portfolios

Professional portfolios can be developed in a variety of contexts including inservice programs, collegial circles, or as part of the evaluation/supervision process. They can be developed through a formal and directed process (the portfolio developer is told what to include and annotate) or in a self-directed and informal process (the portfolio developer identifies the kinds of work that ought to be included and reflects on the work as the opportunity arises).

Portfolios can be developed by individuals or small groups, who can decide on all or some of the artifacts to include. Teachers can develop them to document their learning about curriculum, instruction, and assessments over time. Administrators can develop them to document their learning about teaching, learning, management, and supervision.

Portfolios can also be developed as school districts redesign their teacher evaluation and supervision systems. In this context, teachers and administrators can compile ongoing evidence of their work and use their portfolio as the primary means for communicating with their supervisors.

Finally, professional portfolios can be developed in the context of collaborative inquiry. For example, teachers who participate in school-based action research or collegial circles use collections of their work to explore, reflect upon, and address issues that affect their practice.

Portfolio Structures: A Three-Part Process

To help teachers and administrators begin to think about different kinds of professional portfolios and their purposes, I use a three-part simulation.

Scenario One

I start by asking participants to respond to the following scenario:

> Imagine that you have to leave your current position. You find an ad in the paper that describes what you think is the school district of your dreams. There is an apparent fit between what you value and what district staff want.
>
> However, this district does not want you to send an application with a résumé. Instead, they have asked potential candidates to compile a collection of no more than five artifacts (paper, video, pictures, etc.), that showcase your professional achievement and growth.

I ask participants to identify their five artifacts and their reasons for including them. After a discussion, I ask them what they would have learned from this experience if it were a real situation. Invariably, they agree that this experience would help them to define what they think of as essential evidence of their growth and achievement, and to differentiate the indispensable from the redundant.

The range of artifacts generated by teachers and administrators is quite amazing. Here is a sample of the items:

- Learning styles inventory of students and accompanying activities that show how the teacher addresses multiple learning styles.
- Letters from parents that show appreciation for teachers' efforts and responsiveness to students' needs.
- Lists of professional development activities teachers have participated in, with an explanation of how they have used those activities to refine their teaching.
- Videotapes of classroom activities using cooperative learning to show how teachers organize group instruction.
- Curriculum units that show incorporation of state standards as well as the use of pre- and post-assessments.
- Photo journals depicting classroom activities for a month, showing the range of instructional approaches and classroom activities used.
- Letters from students who have struggled but who end the year having reached high levels of achievement as a testimonial to the teacher's effectiveness.

- Case studies of students, which include profiles of the students' backgrounds, needs, and academic strengths, as well as an analysis of their learning over time as seen in three to five work samples.
- Art work from teachers' and students' portfolios that depicts the variety of media used with students.
- Culminating assessment, scoring rubrics, and graded student samples that show teachers' expertise as assessors and feedback providers.

Both administrators and teachers identify items such as

- Professional articles that show their ability to communicate in writing as well as their professional expertise.
- A statement of their educational philosophy, describing their educational beliefs and values.
- Excerpts from daily planners that show a range of professional activities.
- Newsletters to parents that show their willingness and ability to communicate with parents.
- Computer-generated presentations that illustrate their use of computer-assisted technology.

Administrators also identify items that are intrinsic to their jobs such as

- Teachers' reactions to meetings and workshops that show staff developers' effectiveness in meeting the audience's needs.
- Final reports on program budgets for the year that show fiscal responsibility and management.
- Professional journals showing administrators' reflectivity and thoughtfulness.
- Job maps identifying administrators' roles and responsibilities.

After identifying these artifacts, we discuss their clarity and validity. Which ones can the viewer understand without the author's explanation? Which ones are trustworthy or susceptible to manipulation by the author? We conclude that most of the preceding artifacts require some kind of explanation from the author and that none alone can provide a comprehensive, multidimensional picture of the teacher or administrator. The combination of the artifacts, rather than the individual pieces, when carefully assembled and described, provides a rich portrayal of the author. This portrayal is impossible without some kind of annotation or story. In fact, one of the best ways to think about portfolios is as stories that are illustrated by the artifacts.

Before moving on to the second part of our simulation, I ask participants if they think that their portfolio, given the instructions for its assembly, can be graded or scored. They decide that the reader of the portfolio is the only one who knows what the portfolio should communicate, because the portfolio developers were not given explicit scoring criteria for their portfolio. I also agree that the reader is likely to select the candidate that best matches his or her own perception of the best teacher or administrator, but that other portfolio developers could have met desired criteria had they known about them.

This discussion reveals one of the most important issues about implementing portfolios, namely, that it is much easier to mandate the collection of artifacts than it is to decide what will be assessed, by whom, and in what ways.

Scenario Two

We then move to a second vignette. I explain to participants that the district to which they are applying has posted an ad, just as in the first scenario, but that this ad spells out the portfolio artifacts that participants need to submit for review. These include

- Educational philosophy.
- Three letters, one from a parent, one from a supervisor, and one from a peer—all of which attest to the candidate's ability to communicate effectively with different stakeholders.
- An annotated list of all professional development activities in which the candidate has participated. The annotation should refer to the ways in which the candidate has applied the knowledge and skills acquired.
- An article, chapter, or book published by the candidate.
- A video of the candidate at work.

Next, I ask everyone if they feel more or less relieved with this list than with the requirements in the first scenario. The participants tend to be divided in their responses. Over half of them do not like the list of prescribed artifacts, either because creating them would take much effort or because they do not think that those artifacts truly capture their expertise. A few like the list because they know what is expected from them or because they can easily assemble the required artifacts. We agree that portfolios assembled around the prescribed requirements would be easily scored by the reader, but that the highest scoring portfolio may not belong to the best possible teacher or administrator.

The preceding discussion illuminates another significant issue about using portfolios, namely, that the standardization of artifacts in teachers' or administrators' portfolios can lead to two deleterious consequences. First, these may not be the only or the best artifacts for the outcomes sought by the portfolio reviewers. Second, some candidates may find them difficult to compile or produce because there is a poor match between the requested artifacts and the artifacts that candidates would have selected to display their expertise.

Scenario Three

In the third part of this simulation, I tell teachers and administrators that the ad now requires candidates to assemble a professional portfolio of no more than five artifacts that represent the following outcomes:

- The ability to communicate with a variety of audiences effectively.
- The ability to reflect upon one's practice and to set goals to further one's professional development.
- The ability to identify and use effective curriculums or programs to meet the needs of different kinds of learners.
- The ability to work collaboratively.
- One's best work in the area of assessment or evaluation.

When I ask them how they feel about this list, most say they like having clear expectations for what to include in their portfolio while having the freedom to select appropriate and personally meaningful evidence. I agree that this type of portfolio can also be easily scored and that it can result in the selection of the best candidate for the position.

By using this three-part process, I help teachers and administrators to understand that the most credible portfolios (1) have explicit assessment criteria, and (2) allow the portfolio developer the freedom to identify appropriate evidence.

The extensive range of required knowledge, skills, and dispositions that teachers must demonstrate, along with the range of artifacts that could provide evidence of their attainment, has enhanced my appreciation of what it takes for teachers to deliver effective and rigorous learning experiences for their students. I cannot think of a better vehicle for capturing such evidence than a professional portfolio.

What Do Portfolios Look Like?

Professional portfolios can assume different forms and, as we have seen, contain varied kinds of artifacts. Sometimes they resemble journals that contain narratives about teachers' and administrators' thinking and work. For teachers, these narratives may describe their philosophy and beliefs about learning; the contexts in which they work and their students' characteristics, needs, or experiences develop; and the evolution that they have undergone as a professional or as a learner. They may also address the curriculum, instruction, or assessment demands that teachers face; any particularly pressing concerns; or the questions that frame their professional inquiry. Finally, these narratives might portray the developers' specific learning needs and the kind of response they would like from a reader.

Unlike journals, teacher portfolios also include the objects that frame the teachers' narratives. These objects may include lesson plans, assessment measures, videos of classroom activities or of students' performances, and samples of graded and ungraded student work.

Professional portfolios can be tightly or loosely structured. Tight structures are those in which a teacher or administrator follows a prescribed set of outcomes and kinds of evidence. They result in a purposeful and systematic collection whose primary audience is the person who developed it; however, the collection can also be a communication device for different kinds of readers.

Loose structures are those in which the developer selects the specific outcomes for the portfolio as well as the evidence to be included. This type of structure results in a personal document whose exclusive audience is the person developing the portfolio. For example, when teachers begin to develop and use portfolios with their students, they often use teacher-directed and tightly structured portfolio designs that prescribe the kinds of work that students include, the schedule for including this work, and the kinds of questions students are to reflect upon.

Similarly, when I began to use portfolios, I structured them tightly. I defined the outcomes that would frame the teachers' portfolios, the kinds of work they would include, and the reflective activities they would engage in. Over time, I learned—much as teachers learn by continuing to experiment with student portfolios—to share control in ways that enable teachers to customize their learning without sacrificing my needs for accountability and communication.

To assist teachers and administrators in defining and studying their professional expertise, I have created a taxonomy of portfolios centered around four different areas of specialization: teacher/administrator-as-learner, teacher/administrator-as-researcher, teacher-as-curriculum-and-assessment-developer, and teacher/administrator-as-professional-developer. Each requires very different types of evidence. In Chapters 4–6, we will look at rubrics for these four types of portfolios as well as excerpts from actual portfolios.

These four areas for portfolio development are not mutually exclusive, and educators can be involved in activities that cross over from one area to another. For the most part, however, they will devote much of their energies to one of these areas. Over time, as they gain considerable experience, teachers and administrators may merge different portfolios, or produce more than one. I have had more practice using these types of portfolios and rubrics with teachers, but administrators can use them as well.

Three Examples of Portfolio Development

Before I can explain what I've learned from using professional portfolios, I need to describe the three specific experiences that have led to my understanding of them: the Hudson Valley Portfolio Assessment Project, the Hendrick Hudson School District Portfolio Initiative, and the Hilton School District CLASSIC Initiative. The CLASSIC project illustrates my current work with teachers. Similarly, teachers who might consider developing professional portfolios—either because they feel compelled to for their own professional development or in response to administrative or professional demands—will need to accept the process as evolutionary and situational. I present all the steps on the way because many teachers have benefited from earlier techniques, and because all of these techniques are suitable to different portfolio purposes. The administrators who participated in the Hudson Valley Portfolio Assessment Project and the CLASSIC Initiative selected an area of focus for their portfolio work. In most cases, administrators either developed a portfolio around their staff development efforts or their action research questions.

Hudson Valley Portfolio Assessment Project

The Hudson Valley Portfolio Assessment Project (HVPAP) was a regional initiative led by seven Boards of Cooperative Educational Services (BOCES) in New York from 1993 to 1996.[1] It included 100 teachers from 50 school districts whose goals were to (1) develop and implement alternative student assessments, including student portfolios, performance and authentic assessments, and process assessments; (2) identify regional K–12 standards and exemplars in literacy and communication; and (3) facilitate the learning of teachers in their districts. During each of the project's three years, teachers participated in a week-long summer institute and five full days of professional development throughout the school year. Each year, they developed and shared a portfolio of their work. The project included the following portfolio requirements:

1. Outcomes addressed by student portfolios or performances you are designing. What is the assessment trying to document? What indicators support the attainment of these outcomes? Where does the assessment fit into the overall curriculum?
2. Descriptions of student portfolio or assessment tasks (time line, content focus, participants, kinds of entries—allowed or required?—time devoted to each entry, role of student, parent, etc.). Rubrics and grading devices used to assess the portfolio or performance components, or the portfolio/performance as a whole. (Includes a copy of all the assessment drafts generated during the year.)
3. Profiles of your classroom and school. Salient demographic factors (socioeconomic status, cultural diversity, kind of school, etc.)
4. Profiles of three to five target students. In what ways do these students capture the diversity of your classroom?
5. Descriptions of lessons/activities that precede/lead/follow portfolio or performance entries.
6. Student portfolios/performances or students profiled and additional student work if necessary (especially exemplary work).
7. Dated journal of activities involved in designing and implementing action research project using portfolios. Include comments on
   - Students' reaction to performance with tasks or portfolio entries.

[1] For additional information on the work produced and the lessons learned from the Hudson Valley Portfolio Assessment Project, see Martin-Kniep, G. O., et. al. (1998). *Why am I doing this? Purposeful teaching through portfolio assessment.* Portsmouth, NH: Heinemann.

• Time required to administer/score/comment on portfolio/task (use separate log if necessary).

• Reactions or questions about your use of alternative assessments.

8. Optional entry.

Until the HVPAP I had never experimented with teacher portfolios and, thus, had no models to draw from. Yet, because many of the program participants were developing student portfolios themselves, it made perfect sense to me for them to engage in a process similar to the one they were using with their students. Not only did using portfolios enable them to understand the development process from within, but it also provided a window on their learning about assessment.

I gave the participants a checklist to help them compile and monitor their portfolio assessment work, and program consultants were available to provide teachers with feedback on their work. I developed this checklist by (1) identifying and codifying all the components of the educational programs that teachers used; (2) referring to the literature on assessment; and (3) consulting with experts on curriculum and assessment, including Grant Wiggins, Paul LeMahieu, and Roland Case. I discussed and refined the checklist with the teachers during several of our programs, modeled its use with two program participants, and produced a videotape of the review process for teachers' reference. Teachers used the checklist to compile their portfolios and to engage in yearly peer-review sessions. The HVPAP checklist is in Appendix 1 (p. 85).

In addressing the criteria on the checklist, teachers use a scale of 1–5 ("not at all" to "definitively"). The criteria include outcomes and indicators, standards and criteria, portfolio use, scope of portfolio, portfolio entries, and journal (and/or introductory letter to the reader). Teachers also answer questions about their portfolios, such as strengths, weakness, insights, and implications. Following is an excerpt of this checklist:

Portfolio entries:

_____ The reader understands the context surrounding each of the entries (i.e., coached, homework assignment, individual versus group work, etc.).

_____ The assignments that produce the portfolio entries are described with sufficient detail.

_____ The assignments that produce the portfolio entries are substantive.

_____ The portfolio entries are intrinsically connected to the outcomes and indicators.

_____ The portfolio clearly describes the role that the teacher, students, and/or others had in selecting the portfolio entries.

_____ The portfolio allows for sufficient choice and individualization by students.

_____ The portfolio entries adequately assess authentic learning.

_____ The portfolio entries are likely to sufficiently reveal students' thinking.

_____ The portfolio entries are likely to sufficiently reveal students' development.

_____ The portfolio entries require that the student reflect upon them.

_____ The portfolio entries are likely to enable students from all cultural backgrounds to demonstrate their knowledge and skills.

The checklist had its merits and shortcomings. It articulated very specifically the portfolio inclusions and criteria that would be used to assess them. As a consultant, I was able to give teachers very concrete feedback on their work. I was able to compare portfolios and identify which could be used as models. I was also able to assess the strengths and weaknesses of the HVPAP professional development program and to modify the program based on the data obtained through the portfolios.

On the other hand, because I developed the checklist, and despite my efforts to discuss and refine it based on their feedback, the teachers did not see it as theirs. They had difficulty interpreting some indicators and criteria. In some cases, they had great difficulty packaging their learning according to the checklist. For these reasons, the peer review sessions were hampered, and some teachers felt inadequate about not being able to fully conform to the checklist as they understood it.

Hendrick Hudson School District Portfolio Initiative

The Hendrick Hudson School District Portfolio Initiative was launched by administrative staff from the district itself after members of the teaching and administrative staff participated in the Hudson Valley Portfolio Assessment Project. From 1996–1999, Diane Cunningham, my program associate in Learner-Centered Initiatives, worked with several graduates from HVPAP on a district-based initiative. Specifically, she formed a team of facilitators who worked with faculty from the Hendrick Hudson School District to design classroom portfolios. In this project faculty members also produce a portfolio of their work. The portfolio guidelines and criteria for its development emerged from several brainstorming sessions with participating faculty.

The guidelines for their portfolio development are presented in Appendix 2 (p. 87). As Appendix 2 shows, faculty choose elements that their readers need in order to understand their story, in the areas of context, reflections, portfolio design and related assessments. An excerpt of the guidelines follows:

Reflections

The following types of reflections can provide insight into the **main character** of the story. Combinations of them will more fully develop the main character and will reveal the **conflicts** and **themes** in a portfolio developer's story.

1. A Dear Reader letter that guides the reader through the portfolio and tells the story of its development.
2. The writer's analysis of other strengths as an assessor and her areas for improvement, as well as her goals and plans for further learning.
3. A philosophy statement describing what the writer values and believes in.
4. Selected journal entries that reveal the writer's learning, insights, and struggles about the course content with commentary/analysis.
5. Reflections on/analyses of particular tasks, assessments, and products related to portfolio and authentic assessment.

They also respond to a number of questions that may help them as they assemble their portfolios. Sample questions include:

Some questions to guide *reflection:*

What kind of learner am I? What parts of the project have helped me learn most about assessment?

What goals have I set for myself for assessment and/or reflection in my classroom? Why have I set these goals?

What do I understand about assessment or using student portfolios? What is working? What successes am I having?

What am I confused about/struggling with concerning assessment or the use of student portfolios? What questions do I have?

What do I understand about the role of reflection in assessment or portfolio assessment? What questions do I have?

How are students reacting/interacting with their portfolios? What can they do well? What struggles are they having? How can I address their struggles?

What have I struggled most with this year related to assessment or portfolio assessment? Why?

The complete Hendrick Hudson Teacher/ Administrator-as-Learner Portfolio Rubric is in Appendix 3 (p. 91).

The Hendrick Hudson portfolio guidelines and rubric differ distinctly from the Hudson Valley portfolio checklist. The Hudson Valley checklist provided teachers with precise information on what to include in their portfolios, but did not allow them to customize their portfolio, nor did it clarify the differences among portfolios of different quality or at different developmental stages. In the Hendrick Hudson initiative, we shared exemplars with teachers, who, in turn, used these exemplars and their own insights to generate the criteria for assessing their work. The rubric they generated articulated these criteria and differentiated among portfolios at different stages of development. It also provided them with significant room to personalize their portfolios.

Hilton School District CLASSIC Initiative

The final example illustrates my current work with teachers. The initiative launched by the Hilton School District in 1994 is known as CLASSIC (Curriculum Learning Assessment Initiative for Children). The four major goals of this comprehensive endeavor are to

1. Develop and use appropriate and authentic assessment.
2. Increase reflective practice among teachers.
3. Develop integrated and interdisciplinary curriculum.
4. Align curriculum to district and state standards.

CLASSIC works with staggered cohorts of teachers for three years in the areas of exit outcomes, curriculum design and integration, and

Figure 1.1
Excerpt from CLASSIC Rubric's Goal #2: Emphasis on Reflective Thinking

DIMENSION	4	3	2	1
Goal-Directedness	Goals for curriculum, instruction, and/or assessment practice are specific and derived from a thorough analysis of current performance. Suggestions for self-improvement are clearly linked to a review of the strengths and weaknesses of current work. Proposed goals are ambitious but attainable.	Goals for curriculum, instruction, and/or assessment practice are specific and are linked to current practice. Suggestions for self-improvement are generally related to perceived strengths and weaknesses. Proposed goals are not realistic.	Goals for curriculum, instruction, and/or assessment practice are general and/or unrelated to analysis of current practice. Suggestions for self-improvement and proposed goals are too general or too tentative, and are divorced from stated strengths and weaknesses.	The relationship between perceived goals and current practice cannot be established, either because the analysis is too superficial or has not been completely carried out. Goals are not stated in attainable terms.

—Adapted from rubric developed by the Long Island Performance Assessment Project, 1997.

assessment design. To date, over 70 percent of the staff has been involved in this work, and we continue to add new cohorts every year. Each member of the cohort produces a portfolio at the end of the second year and refines it by the end of the third project year. The audience for the portfolios produced by each cohort is the subsequent cohort of teachers. In CLASSIC, teachers involved in the first cohort developed a scoring rubric to guide the development of their professional collections by examining and adapting rubrics and checklists developed by other initiatives I have led. Because every participating cohort refines it, this rubric is an ongoing tool.

The current version of the rubric is shown in Appendix 4 (p. 95). Figure 1.1 (p. 11) depicts the part of the CLASSIC rubric that refers to increasing reflective practice.

The CLASSIC rubric represents another stage in the evolution of portfolio rubrics and checklists. The rubric itself is comprehensive, addressing the development and alignment of curriculum and assessment, as well as teachers' reflective practices about their design endeavors. It is also part of the fabric of an ambitious districtwide effort in which different teacher cohorts use the rubric to examine their own and one another's work. As the work produced by each cohort is reviewed by the subsequent one, the rubric is revised and enhanced to match a growing understanding of its meaning.

No Single Best Approach

The different portfolio structures and guidelines presented here (and shown in Appendixes 1–4, pp. 85–100) illustrate the dynamic nature of portfolio design. They also underscore that there isn't a single best way to construct a portfolio. Rather, professional portfolios, like student portfolios, are highly contextualized and need to be customized to the needs of both developers and readers.

2 Portfolios for Teachers

Although I am frustrated at times, my portfolio reminds me that I have a goal and that I am working toward instruction that will benefit the most important people . . . students.

—*John Grover, middle school teacher*
Seneca Falls Middle School, Seneca Falls, New York

Some lessons work and some do not. Some lessons work one period and are catastrophes the next. What works with James does not work with Jessica. The question that Samantha asked became the catalyst for incredible insights among everyone in her group. Yet no one else outside that group heard it. Today's current event and most appropriate context-setter for understanding the conflicts in Bosnia is tomorrow's history. Half of the students failed the science test, but there is no time to stop and remedy the situation.

Teachers' daily experiences with students provide them with tremendous opportunities to understand and assess their own practices. Whereas teachers can learn some of the knowledge, skills, and dispositions embedded in teaching in preservice and inservice educational programs, they can become effective teachers only if they fully understand learning from within. Such knowledge comes from a capacity to reflect upon and appreciate their own learning process and that of others.

Why Should Teachers Develop Portfolios?

One reason that teachers benefit from keeping portfolios is that portfolios allow them to take stock of their professional lives. Improving one's teaching requires an ability to capture and reflect upon a moment that has already gone by. Reflection is about treating successful and unsuccessful events as learning opportunities. Such activity is essential for both teachers and learners. Because teaching cannot be stopped as it is happening, portfolios can become a most effective means by which teachers can examine and improve upon their work. They serve as a looking glass into the self, as described by this teacher:

> After 27 years of teaching, keeping a portfolio has allowed me to focus on developing aspects of my teaching and evaluating far beyond what I've done before. With limited time and energy, I now can concentrate on tasks that seemed too overwhelming before. My own growth as a professional educator has gone beyond talking about change to actually effecting it.
>
> —*Clyde Collins, chemistry teacher*
> *Seneca Falls High School, Seneca Falls, New York*

Much of teachers' work occurs in the isolation of the classroom, and most of the professional decisions that teachers make are seldom shared. Another reason for using portfolios is that they can become the primary mechanism through which teachers can break away from the privacy of their work to engage in the discourse of learning. Thus, portfolios ought to be construed as public documents. Unlike the typical codified lesson plans regularly submitted to supervisors, portfolios need to reveal the thinking behind the work. They need to make explicit the processes by which teachers construct curriculum, instruction, and assessment.

Portfolios also provide a more representative and far richer portrayal of teachers' work than typical evaluation procedures. They require teachers to capture and reflect upon moments already gone by, to identify good practice and areas needing improvement. Using portfolios, teachers can act as professionals, illustrating and disseminating the essence of their work. Thus, a third reason portfolios are important is that the further professionalization of teachers requires that they illustrate and disseminate the essence of their work.

What Do Teachers' Portfolios Assess?

Teaching requires knowledge of specific information (i.e., mathematics, history, physics, health). It also demands knowledge of pedagogy, that is, the ability to develop and implement multiple and different learning opportunities that are suitable to learners. Along with knowledge of pedagogy are the pedagogical knowledge and skills that different content areas demand. For example, there are more and less effective strategies of enabling students to acquire different kinds of mathematical skills, and these differ from the various strategies for helping students internalize key historical concepts.

Teachers also need to know about curriculum development: how to configure certain information and skills so that students can understand and use them within the confines of limited time, space, and other resources. Teachers need to know about resources that support their teaching and how to use them effectively. They need to know how to evaluate and monitor student learning. Most important, teachers need to understand learning as a process. They need to know how to adapt teaching and learning experiences to meet the needs of different learners. They need to be flexible and know when to adapt or abandon a specific strategy, all without the benefit of time to ponder these decisions. In many ways, teaching is about managing dissonance and conflict between the known and the unknown, and between the willing and the unwilling learner in a context of predictable and unpredictable interruptions.

It is possible to assess any of the preceding dimensions of teaching in isolation. For example, we can assess teachers' content knowledge by examining tests, professional papers, or teacher-developed curriculum units and accompanying student assessments. We can also assess teachers' pedagogical content and instructional strategies by observing their lessons. We can look at the resources teachers use with students, and we can gather and examine their assessment repertoire. We can even assess the flexibility of their teaching by asking them to describe how they adapt the same lesson or assessment for different students.

Doing all the above requires significantly more than what is commonly done in teacher evaluation and supervision. The predominant model consists of a few impromptu and decontextualized teacher observations preceded or followed by a conference between the observer and the teacher; the observer then prepares a written report. However, even if we did all of the above, we would not capture the essence of teaching. Only professional portfolios approximate the complex, fluid, dynamic, and interactive nature of teaching.

Audiences for Teachers' Portfolios

Teachers' portfolios have three audiences: the teachers themselves, their peers, and administrators.

Teachers

The primary audience for a teacher portfolio is the teacher who prepares the portfolio. Using portfolios, teachers can document the history of their work, their knowledge base, their practice, and their questions. As one teacher put it:

> My first-year portfolio was designed as a learning tool for me. . . . I was the audience. Because of this approach, I had tangible evidence that showed the progression of my own crusade for self-improvement and development as well as my implementation of new instructional skills.
>
> —*Bonnie Keaveny, world history teacher*
> *Red Jacket High School, Manchester, New York*

Teachers can use portfolios to examine the merits and shortcomings of their lessons and the strategies they use to address the myriad issues raised by students, parents, peers, and supervisors. Portfolios can address the dissonance presented by teaching and assessment practices that conflict with their students' needs or interests. They can help teachers monitor the transformation from the lesson-as-planned, to the lesson-as-taught, to the lesson-as-learned. Finally, portfolios can help monitor teachers' attempts to incorporate new knowledge and skills into their professional repertoires. Although much of this work is a private endeavor, teachers, like other professionals, need to engage in a conversation with their colleagues to truly understand and validate their work. Portfolios can serve as a springboard for such discussions.

Peers

Teachers can and should be one another's secondary audience. Teachers learn best from other teachers, provided they can articulate what they think and know in ways that honor their different ways of knowing and thinking. Unfortunately, this type of mutual exchange is not commonplace in schools. The school day is cluttered both structurally and programmatically. In both elementary and secondary schools, there is a dearth of space for thoughtful adult conversation. The roles of teachers and administrators are defined in ways that foster a managerial/labor relationship rather than a relationship among members of an educational community. Administrators and teachers alike complain to and about one another more than they work together to solve problems of mutual concern.

Things are not necessarily better when teachers leave their schools to participate in educational events that purport to enhance their work. Inservice programs rarely account for the diverse needs and educational contexts in which teachers work, and they are often short-lived, single events devoid of some of the primary ingredients that learning requires, such as the opportunity to experiment and receive feedback on these efforts. Teacher talk in these programs is minimal and contrived, rarely allowing those in the conversation to move past surface commentaries. The development and sharing of portfolios can enable teachers to engage in the kinds of conversations with one another that honor what they know and what they have yet to learn.

Administrators

Administrative staff comprise yet another valid audience for teacher portfolios. Portfolios can enable administrators to enter into an ongoing dialogue with a teacher, one that opens the classroom door on a regular basis. The portfolio can be used to discuss teachers' needs, goals, strengths, limitations, and strategies for enhancing current practices. Administrators can use what they've learned from reviewing teachers' portfolios to foster communication among teachers with similar needs, to match faculty with similar interests, or to enable specific teachers to learn from what others already know. In short, administrators can use portfolios to build upon the existing internal capacity within schools, as well as to facilitate the development of adult learning communities. We need more reflection in the culture of schools, more professional communities, and more conversations about the essence of teaching and learning.

The Content of Teachers' Portfolios

As will be evident in Chapters 4–6, teachers can use their portfolios to document the evolution of different areas of their work. These areas include curriculum and assessment development, work in professional development, inquiry/research, and learning as a whole. In addition, teachers can use their portfolios to document their professional history; the questions and concerns that drive their work; their attempts in designing or implementing better or different learning experiences for students; their exploration of critical issues with one or more students or the contexts that surround them; their professional work with colleagues, community members, or supervisors; and their analysis and reflection on professional resources or significant literature.

The usefulness of professional portfolios increases if teachers approach them as living and growing documents of learning rather than passive and static receptacles of work. Having a sense of purpose and audience also contributes to the usefulness of professional portfolios. This does not necessarily mean that the portfolios need to be shared to be useful. However, professional portfolios thrive when teachers work in a community that values the analysis and reflection of professional work and ideas.

3 Portfolios for School Administrators

A portfolio is an engine of reflection. It performs as mirrors do in the physical world. The reflections it creates are in the world of ideas, attitudes, and beliefs. Mirrors reflect what is, honestly and straightforwardly. They can be positioned to give us a different perspective. They focus light in microscopes to allow us a careful examination of our work. In reflecting telescopes, mirrors put us in touch with events that are distant from us in space and time. My portfolio allows for all of this and more. The mirrors of portfolios, when given proper attention and care, allow us to see around the corners of change.

—Kevin Austin, interim principal
Palmyra Elementary School, Palmyra, New York

Developing a teacher's portfolio is a challenging and satisfying task. Constructing a school administrator's portfolio is more difficult, not just because of the time it takes to complete one, but because the reasons for developing one are more elusive than those for developing a teacher's portfolio. Administrative jobs are characterized by many crises, and not so many daily or weekly obligations. The jobs are not tightly scheduled, and there are relatively few predictable routines. Administrators' key stakeholders are teachers, students, parents, board of education members, local and state officials, as well as other administrators. Often their responsibilities involve little decision making but much implementation of board or state or contractual obligations.

Professional development programs for administrators seldom provide for continuity in learning. It is no accident that the attrition rate for administrators in staff development programs is much higher than that of teachers. Teachers can be released from their school responsibilities for a day or more; administrators are never fully released from their responsibilities nor from attending to the crisis of the day.

As a professional developer, I have collected a far smaller percentage of administrators' portfolios than of teachers', even though I urge both parties to keep such a collection. For example, in one of my current three-year professional development programs, I have collected 80 portfolios out of 85 teachers but only 6 portfolios out of 16 administrators. A teacher is almost never called out of a workshop to attend to a crisis in the school; administrators are frequently asked to contact the school or to return because of a problem.

Because many administrators work in an isolating environment, caught between classroom teachers and supervising administrators, it is important for them to construct a portfolio. Portfolios give administrators a way to look at their work, figure out what satisfies or frustrates them, and locate areas where they can be more creative and productive working with teachers. Next we'll look at some specific reasons and methods for developing effective portfolios.

Why Should Administrators Develop Portfolios?

Administrators should develop professional portfolios for many of the same reasons that teachers do. First, if we believe that thoughtfulness is essential in any healthy organization, we must find ways to foster reflection and inquiry among all educational stakeholders, especially those who have a direct impact over the system's operation. Such reflection could help administrators understand their professional strengths and weaknesses and assist them in developing professional goals.

Second, as schools foster the use of student portfolios, and, in many cases, of teacher portfolios, administrators must be knowledgeable about the portfolio process. By developing collections of their own work, administrators will understand the cognitive and time demands of this process, and will enthusiastically create the space and other resources for teachers and students to develop portfolios.

Third, administrative portfolios could serve as exemplars of high-quality instructional leadership. They can assist in anticipating problems, developing short- and long-term goals and strategies, and using data-based decision making. As with teacher portfolios, administrative portfolios can replace traditional forms of evaluation or can be used for hiring purposes.

Evidence and Artifacts in Administrators' Portfolios

The kinds of evidence and supporting artifacts that belong in a portfolio depend on its purpose and audience. There is no minimum or maximum number of items. The degree to which the author has a clear purpose and audience in mind for his or her portfolio determines whether the portfolio will ultimately be tight and clearly articulated or loosely constructed and obscure. Administrators will select different kinds of evidence depending on the uses and purposes for their portfolio at a particular time. Following are some examples. Where appropriate, I have also included excerpts from some of the administrative portfolios I have read.

Philosophy and Vision Statements

Educational philosophies and vision statements can be consolidated into a single statement, forming one section of the portfolio, or they can be subdivided into specific areas including the administrator's vision for teachers, learners, professional growth, and the organization. Next, we will look at the different components of an educational philosophy along with supporting excerpts from administrators' portfolios.

> *Philosophy of education:* Basic beliefs and values about the purposes of education and of schooling.

John Cooper, the assistant superintendent of Canandaigua School District, in New York, has developed a thorough yet succinct educational philosophy, which, in his words, forms "the matters of conscience" that he stands for, believes in, and works toward. An excerpt follows:

> The role of education is to prepare students for the future, their future, and the future of our society. As educators, we must design programs that reflect our community aspirations as well as enable students to lead productive, rewarding lives as they add to the strength of the community. Students must be able to become "all they are capable of being" as they develop their intellect as well as their character.

Philosophy of leadership: Beliefs and values about the role of leaders in the educational community and about the relationship between the leaders and the different stakeholders in the community.

Karen Salvia is a K–5 director of mathematics and reading language arts for the Canandaigua School District, in Canandaigua, New York. Following are some excerpts from her philosophy of leadership as articulated in her portfolio. She developed this philosophy to try to determine the best ways to encourage teachers' growth and learning:

> I believe effective leaders
> - Are learners.
> - Demonstrate knowledge of curriculum and assessment.
> - Understand and model the teaching-learning process.
> - Articulate a clear vision of the program including philosophy and outcomes.
> - Accept different perspectives.
> - Encourage risk-taking and innovation.
> - Secure resources to achieve program goals.

Vision for learners: Beliefs about learning and the learner, including conditions that facilitate and impede learning and the relationship between teachers and learners.

Kevin Austin, an interim school principal in the Palmyra-Macedon Central School District, in Palmyra, New York, has decided to stimulate the use of diversified assessments among his staff. Kevin's vision concerns the role that hands-on learning plays in supporting learning and the role of assessment in supporting educational reforms:

> I believe strongly that learning must involve the learner, incorporate integrated instruction, and provide opportunities to function at all of Bloom's taxonomy levels of cognition.

John Cooper's vision for the learner is centered on what students should know and be able to do. Following are some excerpts from his statement on vision:

> Education must give students the ability to take what they have learned today to help solve the problems of tomorrow. We must not only teach students factual and historical information, but also problem-solving skills. We must encourage creative thought as well as logical thinking. While doing this, we need to help students maintain the excitement, curiosity, and love of learning that characterizes the young child. Children need to learn how to learn, to be continually stimulated and challenged to find answers to their questions and go on to the next step. They must be taught to think, to integrate, to understand, and to prove.

Vision for teachers: Beliefs about teachers and their professional roles, including thoughts on the characterization of teachers' work and its boundaries.

For instance, my vision for teachers guides much of my work with them. I believe that teaching is a true profession, but that the context and structures that frame teachers' work preclude them from enacting such professionalism. Such context and structures include

- Inadequate access to time for thinking and learning while teachers work.
- Insufficient opportunities to enact their professional judgment about students' work and learning in the context of high-stakes assessment.
- Lack of opportunities to develop rigorous teaching and assessment materials.

• Inability to formally teach one another in preservice and inservice settings.

If we want schools to be places for learning and renewal, the preceding conditions are real and ought to be changed. School reform requires a number of conditions and strategies. One of them is to legitimize teachers as professionals.

Vision for curriculum, instruction, and assessment: Beliefs about the nature and quality of the curriculum, teaching approaches, learning experiences, and types and uses of student assessments.

Karen Salvia's strong interest in using assessment as a tool to improve teaching and learning led her to articulate her beliefs and vision for assessment and evaluation in her professional portfolio:

> I see distinct differences among assessment, evaluation, and testing. Testing conjures up traditional methods that require strict standardizing constraints such as limits on time and resources. . . . Teachers view testing as an intrusion on instruction. I see assessment as an ongoing data-gathering process that occurs in the context of normal classroom routines. The information gathered from these episodes helps the teacher and learner modify their actions to accelerate learning. . . . Evaluation is a culmination of the synthesis of data from a variety of contexts and purposes in order to place a judgment on students' performance. With these distinctions in mind, the following statements capture my current beliefs about assessment and evaluation:
>
> • There should be congruence in the teaching-learning process (the written, taught, assessed, and learned curriculums).
> • Assessment and evaluation drive instruction.
> • Evaluation results from analyzing data from a multifaceted assessment approach.
> • Assessment is an ongoing process occurring before, during, and after instruction.
> • Effective evaluation practices provide data that improve instruction.

Kevin Austin has a clear vision for assessment reform in his school, and about the relationship between externally mandated assessments and classroom-based assessment:

> I now believe that assessment reform by teachers is a very powerful tool in understanding and implementing the new Learning Standards, as well as the key to a process of self-evaluation for teachers that has long eluded me. I also believe that the preponderance of state-mandated summative over formative assessment must be reversed and that the use of both authentic instruction and assessment is most important in meeting the social, intellectual, physical, and emotional needs of all developmental levels, not just those of the early adolescent.

Vision for the organization: Beliefs about the organization including how its different elements relate to one another. This vision can be stated as a narrative or developed as an organizational map.

Rob MacNaughton is superintendent of Ramapo Central School District in New York. To develop a clear vision for this district, he used a job map (see Figure 3.1).

Vision for professional growth: Beliefs about teachers and other professionals as learners, including perceived need and support for professional growth and evaluation activities within and outside the school.

Figure 3.1
A Superintendent's Organizational Map Illustrates His Vision for the District

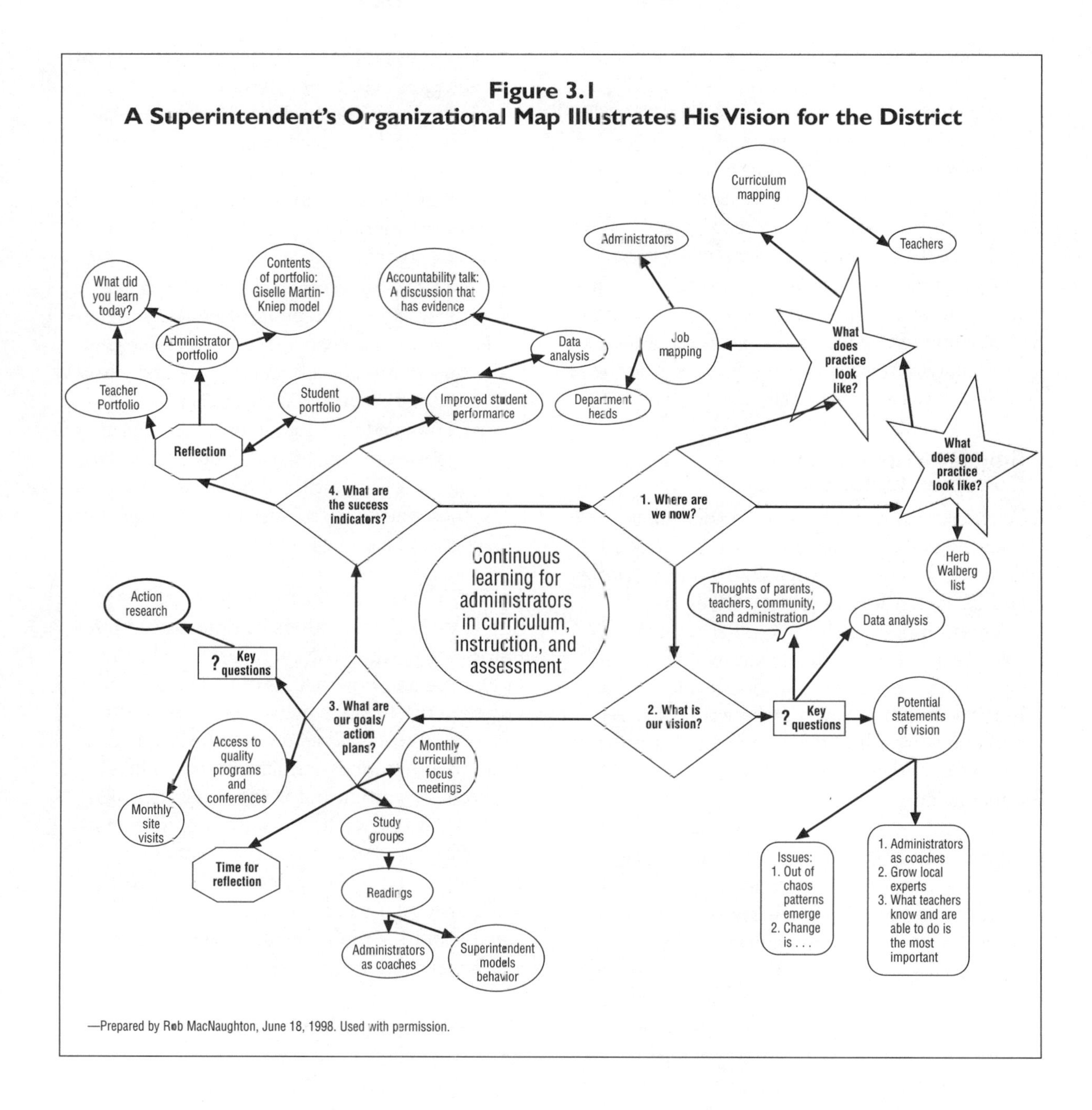

—Prepared by Rob MacNaughton, June 18, 1998. Used with permission.

Christine Mizro, an elementary school principal in the Newark Central School District, in Newark, New York, has had to embrace the worthwhile goal of replacing an inadequate, decontextualized process of teacher supervision and evaluation with teacher-developed professional portfolios. The following excerpt from Christine's vision statement is centered on the role that explicit standards, reflection, and professional portfolios can have in supporting a professional community:

I believe more than ever before that it is critical to address teachers' evaluation issues and make significant changes in order to support the staff in understanding the concept of continuous improvement and the rationale behind the use of rubrics, self-assessment, reflection, and so on, regardless of how they choose to be paid. I also realize that we need to evaluate all teachers against the same standard and in the same manner. If we are using rubrics for teacher evaluation, the process and the rubric should be the same no matter how the teacher chooses to be paid (performance pay or flat rate)!

Role Description and Contextual Information

Whenever the portfolio has a reader other than the portfolio's author, the portfolio should describe the context in which the author works and his or her formal role as well as actual roles and functions, if these differ from the role description. Following are two narratives describing the administrator's role and functions. In the first, Karen Salvia is the writer. The second one is by John LeFave, an assistant principal in Canandaigua School District, in Canandaigua, New York.

As a K–5 director of math and reading language arts I create processes, communicate and facilitate the implementation of initiatives, and provide staff development opportunities aligned to teacher and program needs. I facilitate curriculum development and monitor implementation. I gather program and teacher data, analyze them, and use them to work toward continued improvement. The principal and I meet individually with teachers to share their data and allow them time to reflect on what they do. I also observe and evaluate teachers.

As an assistant principal, I do what my principal expects me to do. An assistant principal gets it from both sides. Normally, the kinds of problems I am asked to solve or issues I am asked to address become somewhat redundant, routine, and predictable. Some of what I do involves higher cortical functioning and my administrative certificate. However, my office is responsible for a lot of tasks and duties other than instructional leadership.

I believe that teachers see me as doing just about everything except instructional leadership for two reasons. First, if their lives are to operate as smoothly as possible and they are to do their best at instructional delivery, teachers need someone to whom to delegate all the other elements of that job description. Second, it does not dawn on many classroom teachers that they could or should come to an "administrator" with questions about teaching and learning.

The mere act of describing one's job description to oneself or to others can provide administrators with greater clarity about the inherent limitations and possibilities of their roles. Clearly, a discrepancy between the administrator's formal roles and actual responsibilities can result in either inner conflicts or in conflicts between the administrator and other members of the organization. In the above quote from his portfolio, John LeFave expresses what he is expected to do, what he does, and why he is sometimes angry and frustrated. This analysis could lead to working out somewhat different and better work arrangements.

Challenges, Demands, and Conflicts

Addressing challenges, demands, and conflicts is particularly important in portfolios to the extent that administrators use their collections to systematically reflect upon their practice, set and monitor goals, and implement short- and long-term strategies for change.

Christine Mizro faces a number of challenges as she tries to implement what appears to be a rather sound educational idea. Many of her problems center around the difficulty in coordinating teacher development and teacher evaluation:

> Even though I think there are great benefits to using teacher portfolios for evaluation, I had many problems with this process. Some teachers gave themselves an *A* across the board and would accept no less from administrators. The issue of "I'm working as hard as I can" seemed to come up often. The realization that quantity does not necessarily equate with quality just didn't seem to be there for some.
>
> The scoring rubric was too ambiguous. Even the administrators found it difficult to provide specific feedback for some of the areas of the rubric. Some teachers found it extremely demanding to self-assess using the rubric. Was the problem the rubric, their lack of experience in this type of assessment, or a combination? I do know that after what I've learned this year, we fell short as a district on the training component of the rubric.

Annalisa Allegro is a coordinator of a state-funded bilingual/ESL technical assistance center and a supervisor of a regional English-as-a-second-language instructional program for Monroe County BOCES #2 in Spencerport, New York. Annalisa has chosen to investigate her own learning as a staff developer and uses her portfolio to study herself in this role. One of the challenges she faces in her work is systemic. The primary program for which she is responsible is loosely coupled; many agencies and stakeholders demand competing strategies and priorities.

> Because the bilingual/ESL technical assistance center is charged with delivering staff development sessions to bilingual education, ESL, and mainstream educators from diverse districts, assessing impact on students is elusive. Content is determined by many sources. There is everything but a linear relationship between staff development and students.

Research Questions

The most important evidence of a professional portfolio being a catalyst for continued learning are the questions that portfolio developers generate during or as a result of developing portfolios. After one year of a less-than-perfect implementation of professional portfolios for teacher evaluation, Christine Mizro decided to continue refining the process. She also decided that these portfolios could help her engage in potentially constructive conversations with her staff about the strategies teachers use to foster students' performance in reading:

> How do I encourage teachers to increase the number of students reaching the reading benchmarks at the end of kindergarten, 1st, and 2nd grades?
>
> At the district level, what actions can I take to focus time, money, and intention on assessment reform as a vehicle for implementing the New York State Standards?

Karen Salvia's research question and supporting action research plan stem from her goal to use assessment as a lever for teacher and student learning:

> How can I better facilitate teachers' skill development and reflection on their literacy practices to continue to improve program achievement levels for all students?
>
> To address this question, I need to consider several questions:
>
> - What are the effective literacy practices in a balanced program as reflected by the literature?
> - What do I currently do to support teachers, and how effective am I in my support?
> - What systems can I put in place to gather teacher needs for skill development/reflection?

- How will I collect, analyze, and use these data to improve program results?
- What teachers will be involved in this project?
- How will I communicate the project and select participants?
- How many participants should be included?

Kevin Austin asks a general but pointed question about his continued role as an instructional leader:

> At the building level, what actions can I take to create a climate and atmosphere that promotes teacher reflection and focuses teachers' attention on assessment practices, specifically increasing the frequency of formative assessments?

Professional portfolios can enable administrators to ponder essential questions about their work. Such questions might include:

- What is worth teaching?
- What is worth learning?
- What is effective professional development?
- How can a school embody a learning community?

Goal Statements and Strategies for Goal Attainment

Administrators' goals flow directly from their vision and challenges, but the precision and articulation of these goals varies from one person to another. Christine Mizro states her goals as action steps for herself:

> 1. I asked to join the rubric revision subcommittee so that I can participate in its refinement.
> 2. I will continue to work toward improving the feedback and follow-up I provide teachers in the mid-year formative evaluation conference.
> 3. I will introduce my goal at the September faculty meeting along with the idea of action research.
> 4. I will use some handouts provided in this workshop.
> 5. I will invite staff to participate as action co-researchers and hand out dialogue journals, inviting them to dialogue with me in writing.
> 6. I will also encourage teachers to develop their own action research plans using the identified focus or a focus of their choice.

Kevin Austin, on the other hand, states his goals by activities accompanied by a time line.

> 1. Assemble materials to provide a series of awareness sessions on authentic assessment for administrative team (target date: July 8, 1997).
> 2. Focus teacher observation program on formative assessment issues (target date: December 1997–April 1998).

Annalisa Allegro's goals and strategies are embedded in a broader context or justification for each goal:

> The focus of many of the ESL meetings during the past year was on instruments and methods for formative and summative assessments that appropriately reflect the process of limited-English-proficient students in acquiring the literacy skills in a second language. However, considering the diverse issues surrounding this topic and the limited practical information available, the implementation of such assessments was an ambitious goal for one year.
>
> A four-day workshop at the end of June is scheduled to provide concentrated time and support for reflective examination of the issues and begin development or modification of authentic assessment tools. During the 1997–98 school year, follow-up sessions will take place, and on-site support will be available to staff as they begin implementation.

As with student portfolios, goals and strategies need to be revisited and reflected upon regularly. It is critical that administrators use their portfolios as a tool to periodically reflect on their progress toward reaching set goals, or on the extent to which new goals have replaced old ones.

Achievements and Accomplishments

A description of the author's professional accomplishments and achievements is necessary if a portfolio is to be a showcase of his or her work. This section could include a curriculum vitae and/or résumé, a description of professional career moves and accomplishments, along with supporting artifacts (i.e., completed reports, board presentations, published articles, etc). These artifacts could be clustered around the different roles that the administrator plays. For example, an administrator could have artifacts that showcase work in curriculum and instruction, assessment development, parent and community interaction, communication with teachers, presentations, professional growth activities, and committee work.

This section of the portfolio could also include testimonials from colleagues, supervisors, teachers, students, parents, or other stakeholders in the educational community.

Audiences for Administrators' Portfolios

As with teachers' and students' portfolios, the portfolio's author is the primary audience for the portfolio. Additional audiences comprise other administrators as well as teachers, who could learn much about what it means to be in an administrative position. Finally, administrators can use some or all of their professional portfolios as they apply for new positions.

Canandaigua School District recently required that candidates for the position of middle school principal develop a principal portfolio. Their portfolio is made up of three parts. Part 1 includes the candidate's credentials, application, and responses to the following five questions:

1. Tell us about your perception of the middle school student. What makes a middle school experience unique?
2. How do you keep in touch with your students so you are fully aware of the issues that are important to them?
3. What are some of the current issues in education that most impact the middle school community?
4. How do you see the role of the team in the middle school?
5. How have you been an active participant in the life of your community?

In Part 2 candidates provide a sample of a long-range plan they helped create; discuss some of the experiences that have shaped their personal beliefs and goals; show how they interact and develop relationships with students; and show how they have fun.

In Part 3 candidates respond to the following four entries:

1. Demonstrate your communication skills and your understanding of the teacher observation process by providing a video of a postobservation conference between you and a teacher or some other depiction of your understanding of those two areas.
2. Bring a copy of a middle or high school schedule, and be prepared to discuss your understanding of scheduling in general and your schedule in particular.
3. Bring a draft of a letter to parents that you would send out prior to your first year as principal in our school. Introduce yourself to the parents and include some of your ideas to help them become more involved in the middle school community.

4. Put together an agenda for the first regular faculty meeting after school opens. Let the agenda reflect your "faculty meeting philosophy." Include your personal goals for the coming year.

Portfolios Serve Several Purposes

When asked to develop professional portfolios, either for supervision and evaluation purposes or as part of the hiring process, administrators need clear guidelines. Preferably, these directions should come with explicit performance criteria and rubrics.

Administrative portfolios used to apply for a job are consistent with the increased perceived value that collections of work have for employment recruiters. In addition to being showcases of professional work, such portfolios provide a valuable learning experience for their authors if they have included annotations that explain their thinking about the work they've included. Without such thinking, the collections are artifacts whose value will depend on the reader's expectations, assumptions, and beliefs.

4 Teacher/Administrator-as-Learner Portfolios

Although portfolios are a valuable assessment tool, they may be equally valuable as an instructional tool, helping teachers and students assume greater ownership over their own learning. I enjoyed the teacher-as-learner concept we used in our first year together. I documented my learning and my growth as a learner. I was encouraged to think about my learning process, with the recognition that people learn differently. Portfolios help remind us that learning is hard work. I hope that my students will also come to appreciate and understand their learning process and to use it to their benefit.

—*Cynthia Shepardson, enrichment supervisor*
Newark Middle School, Newark, New York

It is much easier to be a good student than a good learner, and it is puzzling how the two words share as many differences as they do similarities. Good students are attentive, present, and seemingly interested. They sit quietly, complete the task at hand, respond when asked questions, and are concerned about complying with, and even succeeding at attaining, the expected performance. Good learners are also curious and interested, but they are inquisitive as well. They consider the information presented but question its meaning. They are respectful but not necessarily accepting of a specific viewpoint. They intuitively knows there is more to it. Learners always generate more questions than answers and accept that knowledge is tentative. They are comfortable with ambiguity and understand that learning is a process. Learners are interested in knowing more.

In this chapter, we'll look at portfolios as a vehicle for learning. Although this type of portfolio is helpful for both teachers and administrators, we'll look at it primarily from the perspective of teachers.

Producing learners is a difficult task for teachers. Schools often focus on compliance and end-points, and the material delivered does not provide teachers or students with the open-endedness and inquiry focus needed for them to understand the journey toward the pursuit of deeper knowledge and meaning.

Enabling teachers to develop a learner portfolio entails helping them see the open-endedness of their pursuit to become better teachers. To do so, they must learn to become reflective about their own work in very specific ways. The starting point of this process lies in convincing teachers that their thoughtful analysis of work-in-progress is more valuable than the polished products of their learning. In fact, several drafts of a student assessment or rubric—along with a commentary on the strengths and weaknesses of each draft and the revisions the teacher has made in response to his or her learning—are a stronger indication of a teacher's professionalism than a finished rubric or assessment.

The teacher-as-learner portfolio presents a story of the teacher as a lifelong, reflective learner engaged in making meaning. The teacher shows an awareness of his or her audience by providing sufficient description of the context within which work or learning has taken place as well as of thoughtfulness and reflectivity.

In this chapter I will describe and show what teachers' reflections look like in a teacher-as-learner portfolio. These reflections touch on different aspects of reflective practice: awareness of self; understanding of learning needs, questions, and process; habitual reflective practice; clear goals for changes in practice; and increased appreciation of the nature of qualities of different kinds of changes. As much as possible, teachers' reflections will be in the voices of the teachers themselves.

Figure 4.1 is a description of what an exemplary portfolio looks like. The entire rubric for a teacher/administrator-as-learner portfolio—from undeveloped to emerging to developed to exemplary—is shown in Appendix 5 (p. 101).

Awareness of Self

A learner has a solid grasp of his or her strengths and weaknesses and is not afraid to reveal them. This quality is exemplified by former professional developer Leslie Anderson, who is now a 4th grade teacher in the Hendrick Hudson School District in Montrose, New York.

> Teachers in my district see me as a "task analyst." I am not naturally a very global thinker (I am working on that). It takes me lots of time and work to come up with new creative projects and ideas . . . so I am very proud of myself when I do. I tend to be very left-brained and logical. If a fellow teacher comes up with an inspiring idea, I can sit down and plan out the specifics in a logical step-by-step progression.
>
> I do not "fly by the seat of my pants," but like to have everything well planned in advance. That way, if the lesson begins to take off on an interesting tangent, I can be aware of the intended goals and outcomes for that lesson as I choose whether or not to let us continue along that tangent. Sometimes I do allow my lessons to proceed much differently than originally planned . . . with students leading the way based on their skills, ideas, and enthusiasm . . . but I have confidence that we are headed in a worthwhile direction!

Leslie Anderson's reflection not only reveals some of her strengths and weaknesses but also indicates a strong commitment to question her practice and assert her professional beliefs:

> In my role as assessor I have strengths and areas for improvement. One of my strengths is that I keep asking myself, Why am I asking kids to do this? . . . Is this important enough to spend time on? Is there a balance in the kinds of tasks I ask kids to do? . . . Do the tasks match my standards and indicators? I am also improving in communicating criteria more clearly. Finally, my skill in developing rubrics that kids understand is improving.
>
> An area I need to work on is communicating those standards so that they're not just mine, but that children understand and embrace them. I plan to start next year by asking kids to help me create a list of what excellent readers do, say, think, and feel about reading. Then, each time we do reading, we'll connect the work to these "standards." I also need to give students more ownership and choices. My assessments this year were almost all teacher directed.
>
> I have strong beliefs about teaching and learning. I believe that students want to learn and do well. If I communicate my belief in them effectively, even the most reluctant students will learn. I work hard to communicate three messages I

Figure 4.1
Teacher/Administrator-as-Learner Rubric for an Exemplary Portfolio*

Overall: The portfolio is a coherent story of the teacher/administrator as a lifelong, reflective learner engaged in the process of making meaning. When reviewing the portfolio, the reader gets to know the teacher/administrator whose work and achievements are depicted and can clearly understand her learning. The teacher/administrator is clearly aware of her audience and provides sufficient description of the context within which her work/learning has taken place.

Dear Reader Letter, Journal Entries, and Other Reflective Pieces: The portfolio provides substantial evidence of thoughtfulness and reflectivity. (For teachers, for example, the reflections reveal new insights and questions related to course content—alternative assessments, authenticity, learning theory, student reflection, rubric development, action research—to the application of new concepts to her teaching and assessment practices, and to student reactions to new practices.) The reflections include an assessment of the teacher's/administrator's strengths and areas for improvement as well as a description of her learning process. The teacher/administrator explicitly evaluates the degree to which she has met assessment goals and has set specific and realistic goals to extend her learning. She identifies specific areas where response is needed.

*The entire Teacher/Administrator-as-Learner Portfolio Rubric appears in Appendix 5 (p. 101).

learned from the work of Jonathan Saphier and Robert Gower (1987): (1) this is important, (2) you can do it, and (3) I won't give up on you. I also believe that all people, especially children, should be treated with respect, caring, and dignity. Their thoughts, beliefs, and feelings need to be listened to and understood. If I am clear in my expectations and standards, provide exemplary models and opportunities for self-evaluation and goal setting, students will continually improve.

I need to model what I expect. Hard work, the willingness to look at myself critically and change, being respectful, caring, and a good listener are qualities that support a positive, safe learning environment.

A true learner is very aware of the ideas, people, and events that have shaped their learning and belief system. The following excerpts from Karen Salvia, a former classroom and reading teacher, and a director of K–5 math and reading in Canandaigua, New York, illustrate her keen awareness of past influences:

Over several years I have had unique opportunities to participate in projects that have contributed to my belief system about teaching and learning, literacy development, and leadership.

A collaborative BOCES project with Brian Cambourne, Jan Turbil, and Andrea Butler known as Frameworks shifted my beliefs on reading and learning theory. The conditions of learning changed the way I deliver inservice training.

The work of Stiggins and O'Flahavan increased my knowledge base on the teaching of spelling, word study, and phonics. Developing an inservice program on spelling has been a growth experience as well.

TQM [Total Quality Management] training has helped put many of my learnings into a new framework with an emphasis on data-driven decision making and customer requirements. I really feel the teacher is the key agent in reform. Sharing data with teachers and providing opportunities for self-reflection will be instrumental in establishing classroom environments where the student is seen as a worker who must produce quality products.

Understanding of Learning Needs, Questions, and Process

Teachers who are learners are always seeking to improve upon their practice, even if their practice is already good. Jeanette Atkinson, a 3rd grade teacher in Penfield, New York, illustrates this point by reflecting on how her use of portfolio assessment evolved:

> When I first began to use portfolios in my classroom five years ago, they were completely content-focused. . . . I wanted the portfolios to reflect all aspects of my students' learning. This was in part due to my ego in believing that I could do it all with all my students. . . . It was an overwhelming experience at first wondering what the "right" process was for the children, but I had to start somewhere. After all, the portfolio was unknown territory for me and my students. The children remained very excited about sharing their portfolios with peers, teachers, and parents. . . .
>
> After those first two years, I began to question what those portfolios were really showing about how students learn. . . . Two things became very frustrating: not having a way of providing students with an ongoing portfolio reflection process, and realizing portfolios were not matching the learning that was occurring. . . .
>
> After meeting with the Finger Lakes Alternative Assessment Project in April, I began a sketchy plan for outcome-based portfolios. I asked my students to select four to six pieces that would represent them as learners. They used a brainstormed list of work that would show them as learners. They also set goals for their learning and a plan for reaching them on a regular basis. My most powerful discovery from the changes I introduced was that students became more focused on what could show them as learners on a regular basis. . . .

Jeanette used the following criteria for choosing portfolio entries. She asked her students to select work that

- Was a challenge.
- Shows how you work on a team or in a cooperative group.
- Reflects a goal you have been working on.
- Shows improvement.
- Shows your ability to solve problems.
- Shows how you worked through a process (like writing workshop or scientific experiments).
- Shows your ability to do research on your own.
- Shows how well you can teach someone else.

Jeanette asked her students to make one selection every three weeks. At conferences, they were to display three pieces and to choose one to include in their portfolios. The selection process varied in terms of activities and participants and included the structures for different kinds of rotations. These included:

- Some kids every day.
- Others with kids only (form to report).
- Preconference with kids by me.
- Brainstorm probing question for form to report.

Jeanette asked her students to set goals using the planning sheet shown in Figure 4.2. Figure 4.3 shows a reflection form that Jeanette asked her students to fill out weekly, containing sections for teacher and parent comments.

Figures 4.4 and 4.5 show two examples of student work that illustrate the power of the shifts Jeanette has made in her use of student portfolios. Before using the planning sheet, students tended to put less thought into what to include in their portfolios.

Figure 4.2
Students' Personal Goals Planning Sheet

Personal goals planning sheet of ______________________________

My personal goal focuses on:

____ behavior ____ responsibility
____ learning ____ outcomes

My personal goal is
____
____

My plan for reaching this goal is
____
____

How will I know when I have reached my goal?
____
____

Starting date of goal: ______________________________

Achievement date of goal: ______________________________

Student signature: ______________ Peer reviewer signature: ______________

Teacher signature: ______________ Parent signature: ______________

Teachers or administrators who use learner portfolios see the portfolio as a communication device and as an opportunity to ask for answers to specific questions. Diana Foster, a high school English teacher in Seneca Falls, New York, asked some of the following questions in her first-year portfolio:

- Does my effort at mapping my English curriculum resemble a curriculum map? What would you suggest I add to or remove from this map?
- Do you have any suggestions about ways to help poor and reluctant readers become better and less reluctant readers? I am willing to give up class time to achieve this goal.
- Do you have any suggestions on how to improve the way I deal with journals or ways to streamline the process?
- When I look at the rubrics for authentic and appropriate assessment, I see many categories where my tasks don't measure up. Do all my tasks need to be authentic or appropriate? For example, if I am basing the task on a novel without any cultural diversity, how do I add that to my task? Also, my school community is not culturally diverse, so making my task address this issue may make it not meaningful to students. How do I deal with these issues?
- I do not evaluate my students' portfolios beyond asking the students to complete them because all

Figure 4.3
Students' Reflection Form

Building on Our Learning

WEEKLY REFLECTION

WEEK OF ______________________________

Dear Mom, Dad, and Mrs. Atkinson,

This week I did very well ______________________________

because ______________________________

The most important thing to me this week was ______________________________

because ______________________________

This week I learned ______________________________

I am confused or would like to know more about ______________________________

because ______________________________

I wish I could ______________________________

Love,

* * *

Parent Feedback on Goals/Weekly Reflection

Please reflect on how you think your child is progressing on meeting his or her goal. ______________________________

____

Please reflect on what you are doing at home to support your child's progress in meeting his or her goal.

____

* * *

Reflections Focused on Personal Goals

What did you do this week to work on meeting your goal? ______________________________

____

How do you feel about what you have done? Why? ______________________________

____

What will you do next week to continue to work on meeting your goal? ______________________________

____

Teacher Comments: Parent Comments:

Figure 4.4
3rd Grader Kelly Explains Her Choice of a Portfolio Selection

Name: Kelly Date: 3/3/97

I choose My Nile Story

to show my progress as a writer because First I wrote one story and it wasn't detailed and I didn't like it. The reason I wrote a new story was because I heard other peoples story's they had way more detail and humor so I started a new story, but I bassed my new story on my old one just with detail and humor. I knew I had to change it when I read through my story and there were no good descriptions. So people won't be able to picture pictures in their head.

the writing they choose has already been evaluated. The students compile their portfolios without complaint because it is what they are used to doing. Do you think I need to create my own rubric, or is getting credit for completion enough?

Following are some excerpts from my response to Diana's portfolio questions:

> What you have included does resemble a map and could serve as a foundation for future work. You could enhance it by listing all your outcomes and indicators and then coding what you have included each month according to the outcomes addressed. As currently presented, your map does not allow you to see aspects of what you teach that are essential or redundant, nor does it show how you are making progress introducing or reinforcing certain skills or genres.
>
> I like your reading book list, journal entry, and reading evaluation. Adding a goal-setting entry makes sense. To help reluctant readers, have you considered asking students to brainstorm topics they would like to read about or genres they are interested in and then having the librarian suggest additional books? These approaches may increase the interest level of students who are not too motivated to read in the first place. If you pursue this idea, you could extend it by connecting it to writing. For example, students would write (after reading two to three books on a topic of interest) either a response or a persuasive piece to an audience who would find their insights relevant.

Figure 4.5
3rd Grader Alicia Explains Her Choice of a Portfolio Selection

I choose Sadako and the Thousand Paper Cranes to include in my June portfolio because it showed how I did as a learner because I used lots of different resorres to help me answer some questions.

This shows alot of improvement because at first when we were doing our end project we were all over the place and I got very frustrated.

As we got better the play (our end project) turned out WONDERFUL.

That is why I choose this all. Its all about teamwork.

What I did tried to calm my group down so we can get back on task.

About the journal prompts, what would happen if you listed three to five different kinds of prompts for students and have them select the ones they want to use instead of answering a prescribed prompt each time? How do you model or teach students about quality journal responses?

I am not sure that I know how to make the collaborative quiz more authentic or even if this is necessary. I know that the quizzes need an individual testing/response component. Otherwise, how do you know that individual students know anything? Split your assessment so that each student answers some questions and turns them in before the collaborative quiz. You could also have students contribute an important question/issue about the book to the discussion and, then, record each individual's contribution in the collaborative quiz.

The reading assignments could be more authentic if students were to write a literary review, additional chapter, advertising release, for example, to demonstrate their understanding of the book's essence. Maybe you could try one of these options. Again, I am concerned that most of your assessments are collaborative and that you may not be gathering sufficient information on what individual students know and understand. How do you assess their individual journals?

The autobiography assignment does not have scoring criteria. How do your students know what a good autobiography looks like? How do you model quality writing vis-à-vis quantity?

I don't think that you need an additional portfolio rubric. You may want to collect samples of portfolios that represent different levels of development. You could also add an additional dimension for "reflection" so that you can assess your students' ability to evaluate their writing growth and achievement.

I like the idea of sharing your outcomes with students. It will help them get focused and make your agenda explicit. . . .

Susan Costello, a 7th grade English teacher in Penfield, New York, also poses areas for inquiry and asks questions that reveal her passion for learning:

> I would like to be able to construct a rubric that enables me to evaluate student work honestly without hurting the feelings of my students.
>
> With a rubric, how do you determine what is excellent for a 7th grader, for example, when you consider that a 7th grader probably has a limited amount of experience with certain skills (speaking, for example) compared to a senior, who has had more experience? We know the qualities of an excellent speaker, but how do we determine what is fairly assumed to be excellent for a 7th grader?
>
> Much emphasis is placed on preparing students for life in the 21st century, in the Information Age. How do we determine how much of our current curriculum is the "right stuff," how much needs to go, and what needs to become part of the curriculum?

The questions posed by Susan and Diana demonstrate that both teachers see themselves as ongoing learners.

Habitual Reflective Practice

Like students, teachers are best able to internalize reflection if they engage in this process regularly. This practice is illustrated by Leslie Anderson in the following entries:

> *December 12:* Most afternoons after the kids leave, I slowly straighten the room, then think about my day and what I need to do in the near future. I look over student work. I design lessons and students' self-assessments. I think about this in the car—actually I think obsessively about my students and their learning.
>
> *February 26:* About my own learning. My perfectionism keeps rearing its ugly head. I get frustrated by not being able to do things (know how to set things up so kids know how to choose portfolio pieces); so much needs to be done. How can kids choose the best opinion piece if they don't have models and rubrics with descriptors of levels of success? How can they make thoughtful choices?
>
> About a week before making this entry, I remember sitting at the dining room table on a Sunday afternoon working on my standards/indicators and portfolio entries. I was in tears. I felt like an inadequate *novice,* and I hated it. Why didn't I have a great student portfolio to show? All I had were some abstract standards and indicator statements and a pile of every writing assignment given to that date. It helped to express these feelings at the next portfolio meeting because I was reassured that I was exactly where I should be and that I was putting too much pressure on myself. I realized how hard it is for me when I feel incompetent, confused, or overwhelmed. This entry reminds me that this work is a process and steady progress is the goal.

Andrea Gerstenblatt, a 2nd grade teacher in Farmingdale, New York, shows in her final portfolio reflections an increased comfort for the ongoing nature of the reflective process:

> I feel as if I've reflected so much these past two years that it has truly become a part of me. It has now become natural for me to question, wonder, and search. I suppose I have always been that way, but these two years have forced me to look at myself in a whole new way, and to see what I can accomplish.
>
> I have come full circle to the realization that I really have just begun. I can now walk into my classroom next year with the knowledge that I have made a difference and that I have the ability to continue to do so. This difference will lead me through years of reflection and challenges that I now look forward to with a very different perspective—one that is filled with anticipation and excitement.

Clear Goals for Changes in Practice

Whereas reflective teachers are comfortable with the ongoing nature of learning, they are goal driven and can often set specific targets for their own development. In this next reflection, by Carol Korobow, a 2nd grade reading teacher in the East Meadow School District, in New York, we can see an increased comfort level with ambiguity and with the realization that learning processes do not necessarily follow a clear destination.

> While the destination of our two-year commitment has often appeared vague to me, I nevertheless have learned and acquired some really significant attitudes and approaches to my teaching. I have definitely become more questioning and reflective about what I teach, why am teaching it, and about how I will know what my students got out of it. I now ask my students to tell me what they learned, what was hard for them, and how we can learn it better. Furthermore, I am consciously attempting to become less teacher directed—an easy trap to fall into when you work with remedial students—by "trusting" my students to take charge of their own learning. I ask them, "What can you do about that? Where can you go to solve that problem?"

Lynn Johnson, a primary school teacher at Bloomfield Elementary School in Bloomfield, New York, illustrates her awareness of clear targets for her own professional improvement:

> My assessments in math are criterion referenced but not always "authentic." I need to spend some time on this in the next several years, and have greater confidence in their validity. It will not happen all at once, but I hope to add one or two tasks each year.
>
> In all areas I am beginning to use rubrics more comfortably (with myself as scorer). I need to incorporate more active student involvement in using rubrics for self-assessment. . . .
>
> As a learner in our authentic assessment project this past year, I have bounced from practicing rubrics to curriculum mapping to portfolios to reflections to unit planning to action research, as these topics have been introduced and discussed. *I have not focused on one subject area, but have bounced around with whatever I felt was needed or appropriate at the time.* It has been a year of experimentation! This will be reflected in my portfolio. It is the home for my assorted efforts.

Appreciation of the Different Kinds of Changes

Learners are able to connect their learning across a wide spectrum of their lives. Linda Sykut, a former classroom teacher who is now a special education teacher with middle school students, relates the nature of the changes she has made in her home to her work with students. Following are some excerpts from her thinking:

> *1. The Nursery*
>
> The smallest bedroom has been used as a nursery. It was a wonderful room for a baby and a toddler, and I spent many happy hours rocking, cuddling, reading to my son. Eventually he outgrew it, and moved into the other bedroom, where he could have his own turf. . . . As there were no other babies in need of the nursery, it became little more than a storeroom. Out-of-season clothes, unfinished projects, stuff to hide from visitors, filled every corner.
>
> In anticipation of a reunion with a long-time friend, I was forced to transform the nursery. Reluctantly at first, I stripped the *Sesame Street* mural off the wall. Yellow paint was replaced with white, and delicate blue and yellow border applied. The curtains with their primary colors came down, and lace took their place. A daybed and wicker furniture transformed it into a peaceful refuge, an unexpected outcome of this need to change.
>
> Since then, my friend, and several others, as well as out-of-town family members, have come to visit and use that room. New memories have been added to old.
>
> What did this room teach me?
>
> Sometimes we have to change, not because what we were doing was bad. It could have been wonderful, enjoyable, and successful. But we need to recognize when it no longer works in the present context. New or different circumstances require a new way to use what we have. When we do apply a change, it can result in something equally enjoyable and successful. Just different. After 25 years of teaching, I can recall many activities that were wonderful at the time, but that would not work well in this day and age.
>
> *2. The Den*
>
> My house was built in the '70s. Dark paneling was the order of the day. The house has a den with a double window that looks onto the front porch, letting in only a small amount of daylight. Day or night, the room with its four paneled walls always felt dark and gloomy.
>
> Being a perfectionist, I decided that the paneling *must* be replaced with drywall so that I could wallpaper and lighten the room. When the time came, I discovered that to replace all the paneling meant that all the molding around the windows and doors would no longer fit, as the width of the drywall was bigger than the width of the paneling. This would add considerable expense to the project. . . . A year or two later, as I still struggled with how to solve my problem, I was visiting friends who had painted their paneling. When I had first decided to go with drywall, several people mentioned this alternative, and I casually dismissed it as not good enough. But I decided to take the plunge.
>
> What a shock I was in for! As I stood back and looked at the finished product, I was immediately transported to one of my favorite places: the beach in Maine. The whitewashed-looking paneling was reminiscent of soothing summer trips spent pursuing peace and rejuvenation! In my mind's eye I could hear the sounds of the ocean as it lulled me to sleep.
>
> What awareness did the den lead me to?
>
> Sometimes you don't have to recreate the wheel. What you may choose to replace what you already have may not be as good. Just because it is new doesn't make it better. We can spend a lot of energy fixing something the hard way, when a simpler, easier way may produce better results.
>
> I needed to be shown what could be. I had dismissed the possibility too casually, not giving it enough thought. I needed help (the power of example is a great motivator) to see that another way was better than my own plan.

Linda's essay underscores her maturity in distinguishing among the aspects of our professional practice that need profound change vis-à-vis slight modifications.

Professional reflection results in unanticipated payoffs. As teachers become comfortable with their own introspection, they often transfer those skills to their classroom practices. The following entry, by Ellen Miller, a reading specialist in grades 1–5 at the East Meadow School District, in New York, shows how she has incorporated reflection into her work with students:

> As the second year began, I knew I had to personalize what I was learning to meet my own needs and those of my students. Because I was collaborating with the 4th grade teachers and students in a literature discussion group, I decided to use those students as a focus group. This became my "turning point." In class we further developed our understanding of rubrics, which is also a focus in East Meadow, and we talked about the importance of student and teacher reflection. I knew that these concepts could be integrated easily into my 4th grade program.
>
> As I thought about my expectations for my students and for myself as a teacher, I realized again that I didn't know my students as completely as I wanted to and my students didn't know themselves! I began to include my students much more in the efforts to shape their learning by using ideas discussed during our "circles." Although the students were hesitant at first, I immediately saw the long-term benefits. In addition to these 4th graders, I began to experiment with self-reflection with a group of 2nd graders and a class of 1st graders, prompted by the interest of another teacher, whom I have worked with and collaborated with for several years.

Teachers' capacity to help students reflect is illustrated by the following student entry included in Linda Sykut's portfolio. Specifically, these are excerpts of the student's reflections on her progress toward attaining her IEP goals:

> *Goal #1. Develop and apply strategies to improve reading.* Last year I struggled through a lot of stuff (you learn everything new), and this year because you repeat some of it, it didn't seem as hard. Last year I stopped after every word that I read, and this year I can read a whole sentence without pausing in between. When I read a book with longer chapters, it is hard to remember stuff. When I read a book with shorter chapters, I can tell you everything about it.
>
> My goal to continue to improve in reading while I am in 6th grade is to read outside of school. I want to read *The Diary of Anne Frank* because I am interested in learning about her life. . . .
>
> *Goal #2. Develop and apply strategies to problem solve math concepts.* I am better at my times tables and division facts this year. I only have a problem in times with 12 and 9. Using the times chart, and different color pencils, helps me to get the right answers. I still need help when I do my math homework. Using the calculator to check my answers helps me too.
>
> My goal for next year is to do my math homework on my own. I am willing to stay after school to get help from my math teacher so I can understand it easier. When I am in a small math class, like this year's (10 students), it is easier to concentrate. In a big math class (like 4th grade—22 students) I got embarrassed if the teacher called on me and I didn't know the answer. Plus it was harder to concentrate because it seemed to be noisier.

As teachers increasingly value student reflection, they can use it to further stimulate their own. A portfolio entry from Linda Hughs, an 8th grade English teacher in Manhasset, New York, illustrates this point:

> Amanda's understanding of this project is so clear in her Dear Reader letter. Her mastery of form is evident in the strong paragraph structure, and

her clear explanation of the content of the portfolio shows her attention to detail. . . . Her goals for 8th grade focus on her interest in writing and her understanding of the narrative form. I wish we had had more time to follow through on our narrative writing this year. I am glad to know Amanda wants to work on this genre more. I wish she had commented more about goals in other areas. I am pleased that she has only a few careless errors in grammar, but hope that she masters careful proofreading next year.

I am curious about the *A–F* idea in the comic strip. I found it hard to avoid kids obsessing about their grades. Yet, grades are a big motivator, and I know Amanda was determined to get an *A*. However, I am thrilled that in the end she professes her enthusiasm for the portfolio project. This means a lot to me. . . .

If there is a weakness in my curriculum it is my handling of the reading part of the curriculum. I lean toward kids keeping journals to reflect on their reading experience and their progress as readers, remembering Louise Rosenblatt's assertion that reading is such a private experience, that unless one shares immediate responses the impact of the reading is lost or at least changed. But kids hate to keep journals because it interferes with the flow of reading or it's hard or it's boring or . . . they have lots of excuses. . . . I believe some of their complaints because I keep a reading journal with them, so I have experienced similar frustrations. . . . Another qualifying factor with journals is their assessment; how can I read everyone's journal thoroughly? I did, in fact, read everyone's journal: 10 entries per student. I hate busywork and feel that kids deserve some feedback on their hard work. But it is overwhelming.

Some of the strategies that can assist teachers in becoming more reflective include giving them reflective prompts throughout their participation in professional development opportunities. Prompts such as the following can help teachers hone their understanding and establish targets for change:

- What are your strengths as a classroom assessor?
- What are the most immediate challenges you face in grading students?
- How do you address those challenges currently?
- What do you now understand about curriculum integration that you didn't know before?

Rosemary Paulson, a kindergarten teacher in Levittown, New York, recorded an entry in her journal in response to the prompts:

- What do you now understand about authentic assessment?
- What can you do with that understanding?

Her entry shows how she has internalized certain concepts about assessment and decided on the changes she needs to make in her practice:

> After tonight's class, I understand several factors crucial to authentic assessment. First, a task must be *real*. It is best to have an audience other than yourself. Also, the task should not tap into surface knowledge, but have some depth. In addition, children should be asked to explain what they have learned. Although articulation of knowledge is quite complex, my guess is that even kindergartners will be able to express what they have learned.
>
> I also learned that the task should be embedded into the curriculum. Children should know exactly what the task entails as well as have explicit grading criteria before they begin the task. This factor is very important to me. I can think of numerous times in my own educational career when I did not know the scoring criteria of tasks. The grading criteria were a mystery to me! . . .
>
> My next concrete step is to look at my present curriculum and decide on a unit of study where I can incorporate the use of authentic assessment.

Figure 4.6
A Teacher's Pre- and Post-Concept Map of Her Understanding of Assessment

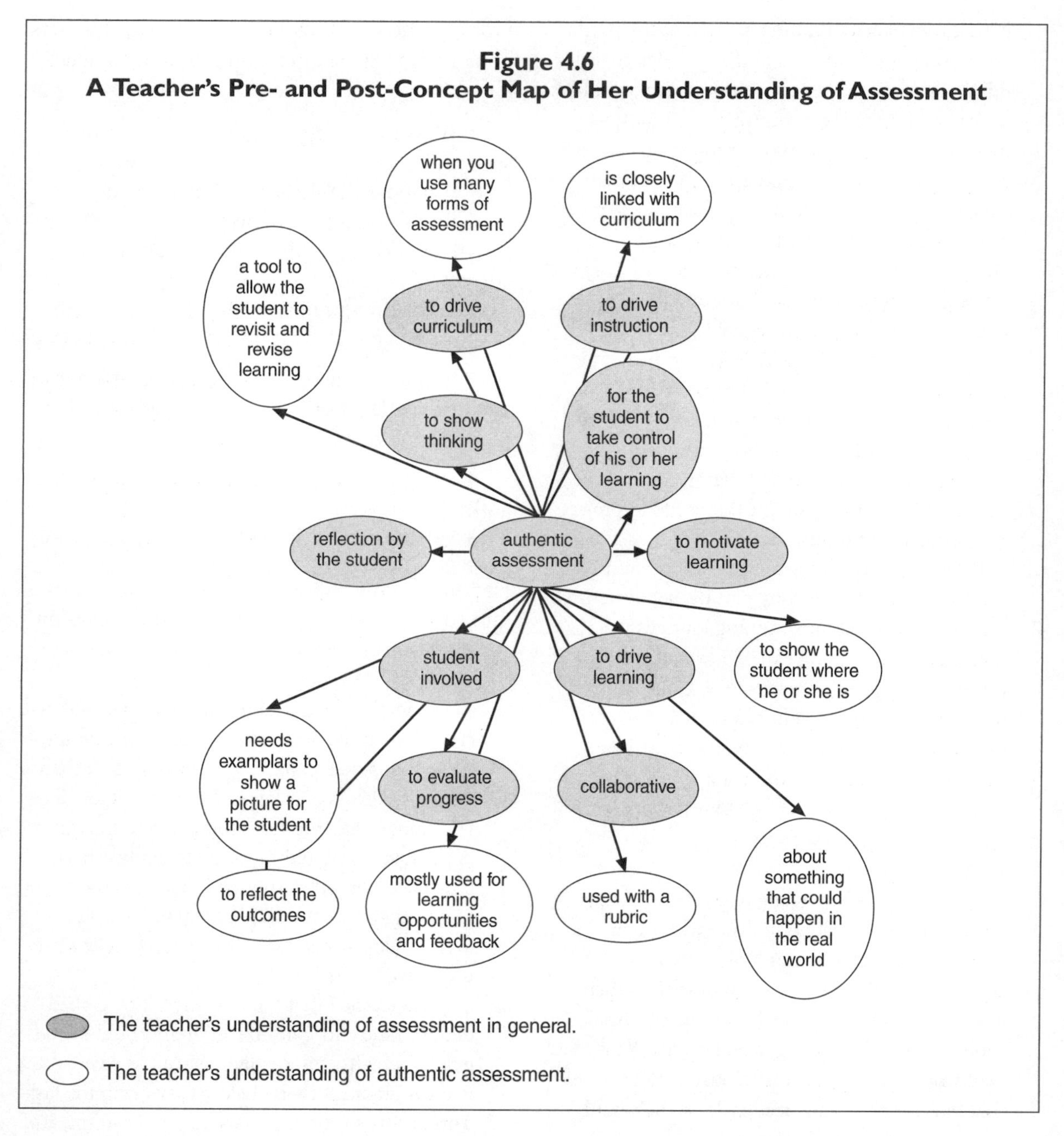

After deciding on the unit, I want to focus on a few targeted outcomes. . . .

Teachers can use ongoing program journals or even computer mapping programs, which allow them visually to examine the changes in their learning. Figure 4.6 shows pre- and post-cognitive map ideas of one teacher's understanding of assessment. As her knowledge of authentic assessment expanded, she enlarged her definition from the terms in the shaded ovals to encompass those in the unshaded ones.

This figure illustrates how the teacher was able to visually map her conceptions of assessment. As she continues to learn about it, she can use them to refine upon future maps.

Professional Reflection Is Key

Becoming a teacher-as-learner is an ongoing and difficult endeavor. Being able to step back to critically examine our practice requires both curiosity and humility. I am convinced that when teachers see themselves as learners, they can, in turn, better understand and foster their own students' learning. This, along with a deeper conception of their professional selves, is the payoff that makes professional reflection a worthwhile pursuit.

5 Teacher-as-Curriculum-and-Assessment-Developer Portfolios

Keeping a portfolio has allowed me the freedom to not be so hard on myself. I have a tendency to do this because I'm a perfectionist and constantly desire to do things better. Portfolio reflections forced me to see the successful steps I have taken to improve instruction. In that sense, it has helped me become a more thoughtful teacher and one who practices what she preaches. As a result of documenting my own progress, I can't deny the things I have done well. So, I have celebrated my teaching a little more.

—Jeanette Atkinson, 3rd grade teacher
Harris Hill Elementary School, Penfield, New York

Perhaps the most important role that teachers play in the classroom is that of curriculum and assessment developers. In this role, teachers design learning experiences that enable students to attain needed knowledge, skills, and dispositions. In many ways, this role is an exercise in translation, for it entails much more than the acquisition or transformation of information. Students arrive in teachers' classrooms with a wide array of prior understandings of their world. Teachers need to help students accommodate and assimilate new information in ways that make sense to each of their students.

Developing curriculum and assessment also entails a careful selection process. I have never met a teacher who does not have too much to teach within an amount of time that never seems to be enough. Perhaps the toughest challenge teachers face is discerning the essential from the nonessential.

As teachers learn about constructivist learning theory, as well as innovations such as whole language, alternative assessment, and curriculum integration, they need to develop or adapt curriculum and assessment experiences to reflect this understanding. Most teachers have very limited time to develop new curriculum during the year or in the summer. Furthermore, much of the learning about these innovations occurs while teachers are teaching. Sometimes externally imposed tests appear to conflict with new practices, or teachers receive mixed messages about the merits of these innovations from either peers or supervisors. It is actually quite remarkable that we see much change in the ways that teachers approach curriculum and assessment, but changes do occur because good teachers are interested in professional growth.

By studying the curriculum and assessment portfolios that teachers have developed in my programs, I have witnessed an exciting array of uses of learner-centered curriculum and assessment practices. In this chapter, I will portray some of these as they would appear in a curriculum-and-assessment-developer portfolio.

This type of portfolio describes the interrelationships among curriculum, instruction, and assessment practices. It reveals the teacher's ability to apply curriculum- and assessment-related concepts and skills to developing lessons, activities, and assessments that target clearly defined outcomes. A typical portfolio might contain some or all of the following elements:

- A letter to the reader that describes the portfolio and its intent.
- A description of the context in which the teacher works.
- A list of the teacher's learning outcomes for his or her students.
- A curriculum map or an outline of the curriculum, which might include key, concepts, skills, topics, or readings addressed.
- A description of assessments that the teacher uses and their relationship to desired student outcomes.
- Samples of student work that illustrate the teacher's curriculum and assessment practices.

In the paragraphs that follow, I will illustrate some of these elements in greater depth. Figure 5.1 is a description of what an exemplary portfolio looks like. The entire rubric for a teacher-as-curriculum-and-assessment-developer portfolio—from undeveloped to emerging to developed to exemplary—appears in Appendix 6 (p. 103).

Context

Curriculum and assessment practices cannot be judged independently of their context. That is, as a reader, I cannot measure the merits of a curriculum unit if I do not know specific information about the target population, including the demographics of the classroom, the range of student needs and abilities, the prerequisite knowledge and skills for the unit, the time and resource requirements of the unit, and the conditions under which the unit will be delivered. Therefore, the portfolio needs to include a thorough description of the context in which a teacher works. Here is an illustration of this contextual information in the school and 5th grade classroom where Kristianna Martindale teaches:

> I have been teaching for 19 years, the last 11 years at the William Sydney Mount Elementary School in the Three Village School District in Stony Brook, New York. Mount School is in an upper middle-class suburban housing development only minutes from Stony Brook University. Approximately 800 students attend Mount.
>
> Last year I taught one of the four regular, self-contained 5th grades. My class was heterogeneously mixed by academic ability, but any formally identified academically gifted students attended one of the two gifted 5th grades at Mount. Of the 11 male and 10 female students in my class, all had similar socioeconomic backgrounds.
>
> Four of my students went to the resource room for academic support. Three went for an hour, five times a week. One student went for an hour, three times a week. The latter student also received speech tutoring for 30 minutes twice a week. In addition, two students received assistance in the math lab for 30 minutes twice a week. One of these two students was also classified as "hearing impaired" and left the classroom for 30 minutes twice a week with a specialist.
>
> I also have a student with a serious medical condition. This student's academic performance was above average, but he was absent for three three-week periods during the year. I also needed to administer medication to this student twice daily.

In addition to the preceding information, this context should provide a clear picture of the teacher's curriculum, including concepts, themes, skills, and assessments and the connections among these elements.

Figure 5.1
Teacher-as-Curriculum-and-Assessment-Developer Rubric for an Exemplary Portfolio*

Overall: The portfolio tells the story of the teacher whose goal is to make instruction and assessment practices one and the same and centered around significant learning outcomes. The portfolio reveals the teacher's outstanding ability to apply curriculum- and assessment-related concepts and skills to the development of lessons, activities, and assessments that target clearly defined outcomes. The teacher has provided all drafts of assessments, allowing the reader to see changes and improvements made to apply design principles and better align curriculum, instruction, and assessment.

Context: The portfolio provides a thorough, clear picture of the teacher's curriculum, including concepts, themes, skills, and assessments. The connections among these elements are obvious and clear. The outcomes around which the curriculum is designed are significant, precisely stated in terms of student learning, and further described with specific and observable indicators.

Assessment Plan (two to three assessments or a student's portfolio): The plan meshes beautifully with the teacher's instruction. The assessments are learning opportunities and vice versa. The descriptions of the assessments are thorough and provide all the needed context, including content area focus, targeted outcomes with indicators, intended purpose, and detailed descriptions of activities that precede and follow the assessments. The reader completely understands how the assessments fit into the curriculum and the roles that teachers, students, parents, and others play in their use. Finally, the amount of time and effort imposed by the assessments is clearly stated.

Portfolio Design: The portfolio design is clearly student-driven and -owned. It has a real purpose and audience and documents student achievement, effort, and growth toward significant and clearly stated outcomes. The reader clearly sees how the portfolio fits into the curriculum and the roles of teachers, students, and others in its development. The teacher clearly describes how students select and reflect upon their work. To evaluate the portfolio, the teacher uses clearly defined and shared performance criteria, which students use in the evaluation process.

Description of Assessments: The assessments are truly authentic. They are curriculum-embedded, substantive, and integrative tasks that require students to build upon prior knowledge, apply knowledge and skills from one or more content areas, express conclusions through elaborate communications, use metacognitive strategies, rethink, and revise. The assessments are valued by audiences outside of school, have a real purpose, and are sufficiently flexible to allow all students choice and opportunity for success. They are relevant to students' lives and sensitive to different needs and cultural backgrounds.

The assessments include measures that guide student reflection on both products and processes that may take the form of specific questions, checklists, or rubrics. Reflections and prompts show the teacher's understanding of the need to accommodate the various developmental levels and learning styles. The teacher has included student work with clear explanations about how the assessments work with different students. The teacher has described the degree to which the target students capture the diversity of the classroom, allowing the reader to draw conclusions about the value of the assessment for wide ranges in student ability and knowledge.

Standards of Performance: The standards of performance for the assessment tasks are clear to everyone. Teacher and students jointly identified and articulated them in rubrics, scoring criteria, and/or exemplars. They effectively guide students in evaluating their work and setting goals for improvement. The rubric design perfectly matches the assessment. Students are able to find the targeted skills at every level on the rubric and can use the levels described to build upon their learning and set specific goals. The lower levels outnumber the higher levels, making the rubric an excellent scaffolding and instructional tool. The top level is above the expected standard—even the highest achiever is challenged to improve. In addition, the rubric includes sample evidence for each level, which the students helped to identify and evaluate.

*The entire Teacher-as-Curriculum-and-Assessment-Developer Portfolio Rubric appears in Appendix 6 (p. 103).

Learning Outcomes/Standards

Learning outcomes/standards are statements that broadly define the knowledge, skills, and dispositions that students should have at the end of a unit, a year, or even at the end of their schooling. In a curriculum-and-assessment-developer portfolio, the outcomes around which the curriculum is designed should be precisely stated in terms of student learning, and further described with specific and observable indicators.

Here are some excerpts from Lisa Boerum's portfolio that provide the context for her curriculum and assessment efforts. Lisa is a special education teacher in Sag Harbor School District, Long Island, New York.

> Because I am a special education teacher, my outcomes are process—rather than content—driven. This information provides me the flexibility I need in a push-in situation. The three outcomes that drive my work and their accompanying indicators are
>
> ***Outcome #1.*** Students will use a variety of communication skills to effectively share knowledge, understanding, and insight about their self-expectations and performance levels.
>
> *Indicator #1.* Accurately describe their strengths and weaknesses on the performance-based projects.
>
> *Indicator #2.* Describe the knowledge, resources, or skills needed to improve their work (classwork, homework, note-taking, and projects).
>
> *Indicator #3.* Use listening, reading, speaking, and writing skills to develop and share their understanding of their own performance levels and to set reasonable goals and strategies to raise their current level of performance.
>
> ***Outcome #2.*** Students will use group- and self-assessments, prior knowledge, and new skills to raise their expectations and performance levels.
>
> *Indicator #1.* Use organizational strategies discussed in class (i.e., time lines, time management, and material management) to identify reasonable expectations for their work and to set goals.
>
> *Indicator #2.* Use rubrics for assigned projects and journal entries to set goals, monitor progress, and evaluate self-expectations.
>
> *Indicator #3.* Reflect after major performance projects on their thinking progress based on scoring rubrics and journal entries.
>
> ***Outcome #3.*** Students will use a variety of resources to gain knowledge, skills, and understandings in order to assess their performance levels accurately.
>
> *Indicator #1.* Use reference materials (textbook, almanac, atlas, and works of literature), prior knowledge, and cooperative group time with peers to gain knowledge, skills, and an understanding of new concepts in order to complete learning tasks.
>
> *Indicator #2.* Use project rubrics to evaluate their performance on each learning task.

To connect her outcomes and indicators, Lisa provides a calendar from the 6th grade teachers in which they list the different topics and assignments taught each month along with the objectives for these topics and assignments. An excerpt from her 6th grade calendar follows:

> January
> 1. Study of Greece
>   a. Build temples
>   b. Solve problems
>   c. Participate in Panhellenic Quiz Bowl
>   d. Participate in assembly
>   e. Engage in skits that reenact myths
>   f. Write and illustrate children's myths
>   g. Engage in a symposium
>   h. Read Greek myths and complete book project
>   i. Participate in the National Geographic Geography Bee

2. Objectives of study
   a. Develop problem-solving skills
   b. Analyze historical quotes
   c. Choose best decision by evaluating results
   d. Evaluate various forms of government
   e. Retell a Greek myth in play form
   f. Recognize audience needs
   g. Illustrate written text
   h. Punctuate dialogue
   i. Create a conflict in a story
   j. Locate countries, regions, and landforms
   k. Self-evaluate

Such a calendar allows teachers to determine the alignment between their learning experiences and their outcomes and objectives.

Curriculum Map

A curriculum map is a matrix or chart that chronologically lists the key content, skills, resources, and even assessments used by a teacher over time. Curriculum maps vary as to the kinds of items mapped, the level of specificity in the description of these items, and the time frame included.

Andrea Gerstenblatt, a 2nd grade teacher in the Farmingdale School District, in New York, developed a curriculum map in which she cross-referenced topics/themes/concepts she addressed, the skills and processes she taught, and the assessments she used. Figure 5.2 is an excerpt from her map.

The map itself is as useful as the teacher's ability to use it and learn from it. Andrea did both as evidenced by the following excerpt:

> The most difficult part of writing my curriculum map was the assessment component. I found myself writing great numbers of assessments, but I also questioned their validity and quantity. I clearly overassessed some topics whereas others had no assessment. I also questioned whether some of my topics were sufficiently connected to my outcomes. Some were and some were not. A problem that we all come across is that many of these topics are required in the curriculum. I need to concentrate on developing relevant assessments for these topics.
>
> One of my goals for my curriculum map was to streamline the assessments and combine some to create fewer, more valuable ones. To make my assessments more appropriate, I first examined my outcomes, specifically in language arts. This helped me develop assessments that crossed over content areas, assessed more than one skill or content, and to develop tasks that my students and I were comfortable using.
>
> . . . My portfolio assessment venture this year has helped me streamline my assessments. The portfolios told me more about what my students knew and could do than the "cute end-of-unit activities" I used to do. . . .

Maps can provide teachers with evidence of what they want to achieve. They can also become the foundation for teachers to make changes in their curriculum, instruction, and assessment based on their experiences with students. For this reason, it is better to think of curriculum maps as works-in-progress than as static documents.

Assessments

A teacher-as-curriculum-and-assessment-developer portfolio also includes an assessment plan that is compatible with the teacher's curriculum and instructional practices. Ideally, the assessments should be so congruent with the learning opportunities that an outsider would find it difficult to discern assessment from curriculum. In other words, students should be

Figure 5.2
Excerpt from a 2nd Grade Language Arts Curriculum Map

November	December	January
Topics/concepts Communities: rural, urban, suburban Poetry Phonics Map symbols Author study: Tomie dePaola Descriptive words	*Topics/concepts* Whales Christmas and Hanukkah Poetry Phonics	*Topics/concepts* Whales Native Americans Natural resources Script: handwriting Fairy tales
Skills and processes Discussions Journal writing Poetry chanting Independent reading Vowel blends Use of adjectives Peer tutoring Show, not tell Reflection	*Skills and processes* Letter writing: friendly letter Discussions: prediction Poetry chanting Journal writing: reflection Appreciation of different cultures Sequencing, retelling, brainstorming	*Skills and processes* Character traits Adjectives, verbs, nouns Using elements of a fairy tale Journal writing, reflection Cooperative work Independent reading Use of compound words
Assessments Journals for reflections on literature Order of spelling words by ABC Locate specific words Work on individual writing Identify symbols on map Create own map Help partner with reading Make up a creative map Locate and list adjectives in literature	*Assessments* Journals for reflection on literature Order of spelling words by ABC Locate specific words Work on individual writing Help partner with reading Write draft of friendly letter Predict and discuss aspects of whales Play various holiday games from different cultures Sequence story and retell Brainstorm what they know, want to know, and have learned	*Assessments* Journals for reflection on literature Order of spelling words by ABC Locate specific words Work on individual writing Write drafts of friendly letter Predict and discuss aspects of whales Brainstorm what they know, want to know, and have learned about Native Americans Compare/contrast fairy tale elements using Venn diagram Share pieces of writing with class for feedback and editing

able to learn from their assessments, and the teacher should be able to extract assessment information from the lessons themselves. The descriptions of the assessments should be thorough and provide all the needed context, including content area, targeted outcomes with indicators, intended purpose, and detailed descriptions of activities that precede and follow the assessments. Readers would be able to understand how the assessments fit into the curriculum and the roles that teachers, students, parents, and others play in their use. Finally, the amount of time and effort imposed by the assessments should be clearly stated.

A 4th Grade Mathematics Problem-Solving Project

Warren Whitney, a 4th grade teacher in the North Shore School District, in Glen Head, New York, focused his professional portfolio on the design of classroom assessments that targeted problem solving in mathematics. After developing a thorough map of his outcomes and indicators, he aligned his assessment design activities with specific outcomes. These related to developing students' abilities to solve problems, apply mathematical strategies, and present mathematical information. Following is an excerpt from his curriculum and assessment design portfolio:

> I presented new problems to the class every week. The students' work on a problem was divided into four categories. In *understanding,* the student explored what the problem was asking for, what information was needed, and what would be a reasonable answer. *Explanation* encompassed all the thoughts, plans, and trials that went into solving a problem. The student then used the *presentation* to explain the methods and answers in words (the explanation) and in graphic form (the representation). Finally, in the *extension,* the student attempted to draw conclusions from his or her answers and apply them to general situations.
>
> Students will work on one problem per week until they complete them in rough plan form. Once a month, students will select one of the problems to "publish." They will select, edit, and polish the drafts. The 10 monthly polished copies will be assessed based on a rubric we develop as a class and will be kept in a problem-solving portfolio. Student conferences will concentrate on defining with the students where each category of the "published" problem solving fits on the rubric. Students will first self-assess their work, then discuss their conclusions with me, and finally set goals for their next problem-solving activities.

Figure 5.3 shows Warren's problem-solving rubric for mathematics.

Warren asked his students to solve this problem: *Mrs. Lopez rented eight dozen chairs for a meeting. How many rows of chairs can she make if she puts eight chairs in each row?*

Here's how one student, Seema, wrote her understanding of the problem:

> *I know (from text):*
> I know that Mrs. Lopez rented 8 dozen chairs for a meeting.
> *I know (from myself):*
> I know that the problem doesn't say the shape of the room.
> *I want to know (from text):*
> I want to know how many rows she can make if each row has 8 chairs.
> *I want to know (from myself):*
> I want to know how many rows you can make if the room is a circle.
> *Assumption:*
> I assume it will not make a difference.

Seema's Explanation for the problem was as follows:

> Mrs. Lopez can have 12 rows of chairs if she has 8 chairs in each row. There are 12 columns and 8 rows so I made a 12 by 8 rectangle. I made a table to show how I solved the problem. There were 96 chairs in all so $8 \times 12 = 96$ and there are 96 chairs on my table.

Seema's Extension to the chair problem is:

> My extension is how many rows would there be if the room was a circle and chairs were different sizes?

Seema's Extension/Explanation follows:

> On my extension I got 12 rows again. I thought it would be the same as before because as long as you have 8 dozen chairs and 8 have to be in each

Figure 5.3
Problem-Solving Rubric for a 4th Grade Mathematics Class

Dimension	1	2	3	4
Understanding	Did not understand the problem	Understood enough to solve part of the problem	Understood the entire problem	Found special factors that affected solving the problem
Explanation	Gave no explanation	Explained the problem, but the reader had to fill in some steps	Explained all the solving steps used	The explanation contained extra information about what the problem solver is thinking
Representation	Provided no representation	The reader had to fill in some details to understand the representation	Representation was clear, organized, and well labeled	Representation showed sophistication (used one or two completely different representations)
Extension	Provided no extension	Provided some comments about the problem	Applied the solution to another area of the problem	The extension reached a general rule (or conclusion) about the problem
Overall presentation	Final copy was sloppy and unorganized	Took some care to make a neat and organized final copy	Final copy was in script, neat, and was colorful	Final copy was neat, colorful, in script, and had special features

row you will always get 12 rows. I also found out that to make it work the spaces between the chairs have to be different too.

Portfolios in a 6th Grade Class

In addition to performance assessments, teachers often design portfolios for their students to use. As teachers become increasingly comfortable using them, their design shifts from being teacher-centered to student-driven and owned. The portfolios shift from being documents for teachers' exclusive use to having real purposes and audiences beyond the assignment of credits or grades. They also document student achievement, effort, and growth toward significant and clearly stated outcomes. The reader of these portfolios can clearly see how the portfolio fits into the curriculum and the roles of teachers, students, and others in its development. These portfolios should include a clear description of how students select and reflect upon their work, as well as how the teacher and students evaluate the portfolio.

Lisa Boerum, a special education teacher, and Bonnie Burke, a 6th grade teacher, both in the Sag Harbor School District, in Sag Harbor, New York, designed a student-driven portfolio for the students in Bonnie's class. Their professional portfolio focused on enabling students to demonstrate their growth and achievement as researchers, creative thinkers, readers, and oral presenters. Students, in turn, selected two of these outcomes for their own portfolios.

To provide evidence of their growth and achievement, students selected two entries for each of these two areas—an early entry and a later parallel project—to give evidence of progress. Throughout the year, the two teachers provided students with a number of assessment tools that students could use to assess their work and decide upon the work that would showcase their learning. One of these tools was a portfolio web, which enabled students to visually identify the relationship between specific assignments and the four portfolio outcomes (Figure 5.4).

We also gave them a comprehensive list of projects that would demonstrate the different outcomes—for example, book projects, speeches, relief maps, political cartoons, skits, tests, posters, and lessons. In their presentations, students must explain how the project demonstrates their strength as a learner in a particular category (research, reading, oral presentation, or creative thinker). Students may use projects from any of their classes; these are just a few examples.

Other tools included self-assessment and reflection questions that students would com-

Figure 5.4
A Project Web Developed by a 6th Grade Class

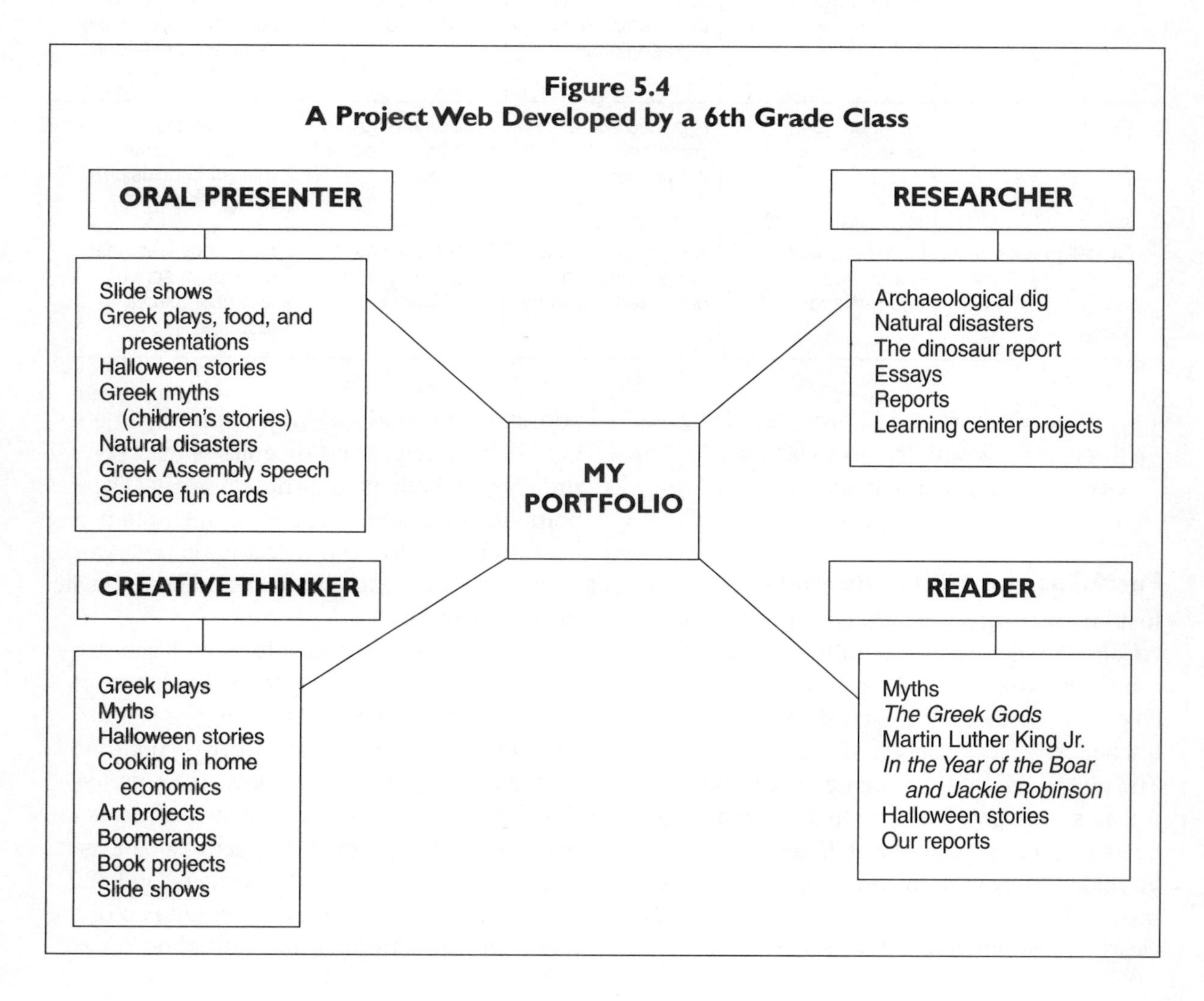

plete on a regular basis. Here are some sample questions:

- How have you used the project guidelines to help you complete the required tasks to the best of your ability?
- How have you used your own thinking to complete the work to the best of your ability?
- How have your attitudes and work habits helped you?
- How have your attitudes and work habits prevented you from completing this work to the best of your ability?
- What decisions have you made that have led to obstacles in completing your project? How did you overcome these obstacles?
- Which methods of gathering information were the most useful to you?
- How have you assisted other students in answering questions, solving problems, and so forth?

For each portfolio entry, students provide thorough contextual information. Figure 5.5 lists all the requirements that students need to fulfill when they select an entry for their portfolio. Figure 5.6 lists questions that students should reflect on after they've selected projects for their portfolios.

As can be seen from the guidelines in Figure 5.5, students in Lisa and Bonnie's class assume primary responsibility for annotating and

Figure 5.5
Guidelines for 6th Graders in Selecting Portfolio Entries

Resources

To help you evaluate your work more clearly, we have enclosed the following in each section:

1. A list of skills or qualities that 6th grade students may use for a variety of projects.
2. A list of possible project from the school year from which to choose your portfolio pieces.

Procedure

1. Look through the list of skills and projects carefully.
2. Decide which skills or qualities are evident in each of the projects you have selected.
   a. Make a list of skills evident for each project.
   b. Decide if the evidence illustrates a strength, a weakness, or something that is improving.
   c. Explain how or why you know this.
3. Meet with Ms. Burke or Ms. Boerum to discuss your selections and the evidence they provide to show you are an emerging learner.
4. From the discussion, pick the appropriate reflection prompts that will help you explain your strengths and weaknesses and how you feel you have improved throughout the year.
5. Take time to carefully answer your reflective questions in complete sentences.
6. Review your responses with Ms. Burke or Ms. Boerum to see if you have provided the evidence of your skills, processes, and progress in thinking.
7. Store your selected pieces, rubrics, lists of skills, and self-assessments in your portfolio.

You may revise your portfolio selections anytime you think another project gives better evidence of your skills as an emergent learner.

—Created by L. Boerum and B. Burke. Ed. by L. Ruhl. Printed with permission.

Figure 5.6
Questions to Guide 6th Graders' Reflections on Their Portfolio Selections

Once you have selected your projects for your portfolio, you will be analyzing your learning process by using the reflection questions provided here. These questions are designed to help you explain

1. How you went about developing the piece.
2. Your strengths and weaknesses.
3. What was easy and what was hard about completing the project.
4. How you revised your work.
5. How you could make your work better.
6. What you have improved on since the beginning of the year, along with evidence in your reflections to show it.
7. How you think your ability to reflect has improved since the beginning of the year along with evidence to show it.
8. How you think your group worked on the project, and how you think the work could have been better.
9. The resources you used to complete the project.
10. Why you selected the projects you did for your portfolio.
11. What the portfolio pieces say about you as a learner.

You need not limit yourself to these questions. Share any insights you wish about your pieces: what you liked and didn't like, what you feel good about, or what frustrated you about completing the pieces.

It may be helpful to reread the reflections you have already written on the pieces. Then you can write about how well you think you described the skills you used and the processes you went through in completing the project. You may also want to explain how your expectations of your own learning have increased. Are you a more capable learner now? If so, what evidence can you provide to show the increase in your capabilities?

Each completed section of your portfolio should include

1. Selected projects that show evidence of you as an emergent/developing learner in each area.
2. The rubrics for the projects.
3. A description of each project, its parts from beginning to end, and an explanation of your role in the project.
4. The skills that are evident in each project:
   - Which are strengths? How can you tell?
   - Which need more work? How can you tell?
   - Which have improved? How can you tell?
5. All the self-reflections you wrote about each project: your process, your performance, your goals for improving your skills, and your strategies for meeting or attaining those goals for future projects.
6. All the materials you and the teacher generated that are related to the projects selected for each section of your portfolio.

—Created by L. Boerum and B. Burke. Printed with permission

explaining the pieces in their portfolios. With such information, any reader can appreciate the amount of effort, time, and support that each student received to produce the work he or she has included.

In their most evolved stage, the assessments within the teacher's and students' portfolios are truly authentic. That is, they have the following attributes:

• They are curriculum-embedded, substantive tasks that require students to build upon prior knowledge, apply knowledge and skills from one or more content areas, express conclusions through elaborate communications, and require reflection and revision.

• They are valued by audiences outside of school, have a real purpose for students and teachers, and are sufficiently flexible to allow all students choice and opportunity for success.

• They are sensitive to different needs and cultural backgrounds.

• The standards of performance for the assessment tasks are clear to everyone. The teacher and students jointly identified and articulated them in the rubrics, scoring criteria, and exemplars. They effectively guide students in evaluating their work and setting goals for improvement.

• The rubric that supports the authentic task perfectly matches the assessment. Students can find the targeted skills at every level on the rubric and use the levels described to build upon their learning and set specific goals. The lower levels outnumber the higher levels, making the rubric an excellent scaffolding and instructional tool. The top level is above the expected standard—even the highest achiever is challenged to improve. In addition, the rubric includes sample evidence for each level, which the students helped to identify and evaluate.

Next we'll look at several examples of authentic tasks, rubrics, and accompanying reflections that I have selected from various teacher portfolios.

A Book Project Assignment in 6th Grade Language Arts

Our next example is a book project assignment, taken from Lisa Boerum and Bonnie Burke's portfolio. Here are their directions to students:

All students must complete at least one project for the book they are reading. Students who have read the same book may work with other students if they choose, but they will be responsible for the choices that they make. The quality of the project should improve if two or more students work together. Students who help other students complete their project will be given extra credit based on effort for that help. Students should carefully read the rubric before completing the project. When their project is completed, they must use that rubric to assess it.

Of the suggested projects that follow, select one to complete. If a student has an idea for an alternative project, Ms. Burke must approve it before students can work on it.

Video or perform live . . .

(3- to 10-minute-long segment)

• *Talk show.* As the host, you should have guests from the book or experts who have insight into the story's conflict. You may ask your audience to share similar experiences.

• *Scene.* Perform a scene from the book that shows the turning point of the conflict. Include an introduction to fill the viewer in on the conflict.

• *News broadcast.* Perform a news broadcast that explores the writing process of the book. Remember to include information about the research needed to write the book.

• *Short story.* If you are reading a series of short stories, write and perform a scene that includes the different characters as if they were to meet. The attributes should remain as they were in their original story.

• *Dance or music video.* Perform a dance or music video that shows the main conflict of the story, complications, turning point, and resolution. Do not use any words.

• *Song.* Write or perform a song about the theme of the story.

Draw, Paint, or Sculpt . . .

(You will need to present your project and defend it to the class.)

• Create a work of art that illustrates the main conflict of the story and the resolution.

• Create a work of art that illustrates the main characters. You should include information about the characters' attributes.

• Make a board game that includes elements of the story. The player should not have to read the book to play the game. Remember to include packaging and directions.

Write . . .

• Write and illustrate a children's book that tells the story to a younger audience. Take your time with your illustrations, and consider the medium you are working with.

• Assemble a scrapbook of the notes and research clippings that the author might have put together to complete the book. Include five entries of a diary the author could have kept to share about the writing process.

• Write a computer game and set up the program to be compatible with a computer in our school. The game should challenge players to answer questions about the literary elements of the book.

Whatever project you choose to complete, remember to read the rubric!

A rating sheet for the book project just described appears in Figure 5.7. The rating sheet is completed by both the teacher and student as the students work on their book projects. The teacher uses the rubric (Figure 5.8) as she translates the ratings into a grade.

Unlike in typical book assignments, Lisa and Bonnie are mindful of the importance of creating products that have value in the outside world. They provide students with opportunities to use their preferred learning styles and intelligences.

Journey Through the Western Hemisphere in a 5th Grade Class

Another example of authentic assessments and reflections comes from Kristianna Martindale's portfolio. She is the 5th grade teacher I described earlier who assigns an interdisciplinary geography and language arts-based assessment for her students. The assessment was developed in conjunction with a fellow 5th grade teacher, Stu Dick, and was assigned to both Kristianna's and Stu's classes. Here are the directions for the assignment:

Over the past few weeks our two classes spent a lot of time developing this exciting project. Keep in mind that you thought of just about everything. As a matter of fact we believe that your ideas are better than ours! There are so many different and wonderful ideas involved. You will be working on a team, doing a lot of research, using all the steps of the writing process, and much more! We expect you all to do your absolute best when working on this project!

Here are the requirements that you developed:

1. You and your partners will write a story about a journey from one location in the Western Hemisphere to another.

2. You and your partners will choose one location as a starting point and one as a destination. The distance from one location to another will be a minimum of 2,000 miles. One of us will need to approve your choice.

3. Your story may have fictional characters, but everything they see or encounter must be based on facts learned from your research. In other words, your story must be realistic.

4. As in all good stories, your characters need to overcome problems.

5. Your team must pick a time period for your travels so that you know the type of people you are going to meet and describe how they live.

6. Your team must use a minimum of three modes of transportation along your journey.

7. Your team must encounter a minimum of two types of indigenous people.

8. Your team must discuss the surroundings of your characters, including geographical features, climate, and so on. You will need to do a lot of research.

Figure 5.7
Rating Sheet for Book Projects in 6th Grade Language Arts

Student	Teacher		
______	______	**1** =	The student submitted a proposal that described a plan of the process needed to complete the project—including information about time, supplies, and resources needed—and included a prediction about his or her learning.
______	______	**2** =	Throughout the project the student communicated an understanding of the research process that the author used to complete the book.
______	______	**3** =	The project was appropriate for the book.
______	______	**4** =	The student presented the project in a clear manner.
______	______	**5** =	The project was neat, organized, and clear. The student took advantage of the medium in which he or she worked by using it in the intended manner.
______	______	**6** =	The student thoughtfully assesses his or her own project by using examples to describe its strengths and weaknesses.
______	______	**7** =	The student considered the audience and followed the assignment's directions.
______	______	**8** =	Throughout the project, the student communicated an understanding of the literary elements of the story (plot, theme, character, setting, conflict, turning point, resolution, etc.).
______	______	**9** =	The student managed his or her time in order to meet project deadlines.
______	______	**10** =	The project demonstrated creativity.

Directions: Rate your project and the process put into completing it. Read each objective carefully. Rate yourself 5–0. 5 = Excellent, 0 = Poor.

Comments: ____

____

____

9. Your team will draw a map of the journey.

10. Your team will write in a journal at the end of each work session. In this journal you and your teammates will write about what you learned and accomplished for each work session. Also, you will reflect upon how you worked as a team and what you need to do to improve your teamwork.

If you want to do something that does not go along with these requirements, talk to either of us, and we'll discuss whether or not we can approve your idea. Please keep in mind that you came up with this product. We both think this is a wonderful opportunity for you to be as creative as possible and enjoy learning about this exciting part of the world. We know you will enjoy it!

Sincerely,
Ms. Martindale and Mr. Dick

The rubric and reflective questions for the Western Hemisphere Project are in Figure 5.9 and Figure 5.10.

It is not always easy to create all the conditions for students to appreciate the meaning and

Figure 5.8
Rubric for Book Projects in 6th Grade Language Arts

A+ The student
- Submitted a detailed proposal sheet describing the process, supplies, and resources needed to complete the project.
- Completed an appropriate project for the book read.
- Communicated throughout the project an understanding of the research that took place and information about the literary elements in the book (plot, conflict, complications, turning point, resolution, theme, characters, etc.).
- Managed his or her time efficiently by considering work arrangements in advance (partnership, supplies, location, resources, time, etc.).
- Considered the audience of the project.
- Completed a final project that was neat, organized, and clear.
- Presented the project in a clear manner.
- Thoughtfully assessed his or her own work by describing the project's strengths and weaknesses.

A Very similar to that of an A+. The project reflected an understanding of the literary elements of the book and the process needed to complete the book. The student completed it in an efficient manner.

B This project was done very well. The student
- Assessed his or her own work by using examples to describe its strengths and weaknesses.
- Could have further developed some elements of the project.
- May not have understood all the elements of the book or did not understand how to use the medium correctly.

C This project had some qualities that were done well, but overall its quality was poor. The student
- Did not use the project to communicate the literary elements of the book or the process needed to write the book.
- Submitted a project that did not match the book that the student read.
- Neglected to hand in a detailed proposal of the project.
- Did not meet the deadlines for completing the project.
- Chose to work with people who could not meet or did not work together effectively.
- Submitted a final product that was sloppy, unorganized, and confused.
- Presented the project in a rushed, unclear manner.
- Could not describe the project's strengths and weaknesses.

F This project did not follow the guidelines of the assignment or was not done at all.

value of their work outside the classroom. Some teachers provide such meaning either by developing tasks whose meaning outside the school is obvious or by developing conditions in the classroom that approximate real-life demands.

A Newspaper Ad Project in an Elementary School

Joanne Picone-Zocchia, an elementary language specialist in the West Islip School District, in West Islip, New York, developed an interdisciplinary mathematics and language arts assignment using the classified section of a newspaper. Her assignment for her 6th graders follows:

Using the business and classified sections of your newspaper, do the following:

1. Uh-oh! You've lost your job. Go to the classified section and find a new one. Cut out the ad and paste it in the space provided. Remember that you

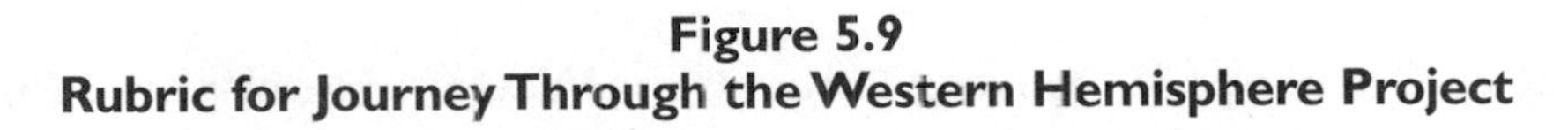

Figure 5.9
Rubric for Journey Through the Western Hemisphere Project

4	=	The journey is completely historically and geographically accurate and true to the time period. It is abundantly clear that much research was completed before creating the journey, and the research is creatively embedded throughout the story. The journey follows a logical story line and is fun and exciting to read or listen to.
3	=	Most of the journey's geographical, historical, and time period information is accurate. The research completed before creating the journey is evident in the story and communicated clearly. The journey follows a logical story line.
2	=	The journey follows a logical story line. Some of the research completed before creating the journey is either not communicated accurately, or it is unclear OR Most research is accurate and communicated clearly, but the story line is illogical and difficult to follow.
1	=	The journey makes serious errors in relating historical, geographical, or time period information. The journey displays little or no research that may have been completed before creating it. It is impossible to follow the story line of the journey, and it is uninteresting to read or listen to.

must earn enough to survive. Figure your weekly and monthly salaries:

- Weekly salary: ______
- Monthly salary: ______

2. Your new job means that you must find another place to live. You decide to rent for the time being until you get to know the area better. Find yourself an apartment, house, or room to rent (subtract your monthly rent from your monthly pay to be sure that your rent isn't more than you can afford—show your computations.) In the space below, cut out and paste the ad for your new home:

   ____ Monthly salary
– ____ Monthly rent
= ________

3. You'll need a car to get to and from your job. find a reliable and reasonably priced automobile. To figure out your monthly payments, divided the price of the car by 36. Subtract that amount from what's left every month after you pay your rent. In the space that follows, glue the car ad and show all your computations.

After completing the project, students answer these questions:

- How did you feel while doing this assignment?
- What part of the assignment was the most difficult for you? The easiest? The most fun?
- If you had the opportunity to do this assignment over, what would you do differently?
- What are the most important things you learned?

Figure 5.11 shows the rubric for this project, which was developed by Joanne's students as they pondered how they would judge their success in finding a job and budgeting their resources.

Presentations in a 7th Grade Class

Linda Hughs is a 7th grade teacher in the Manhasset School District, in Manhasset, New York. She sought to make her students' presentations more meaningful and authentic by having them create a simulated setting for presenting their

Figure 5.10
Reflective Questions for Journey Through the Western Hemisphere Project

Name: ____

Date: ____

Group name: ____

Please reflect upon today's work session, and answer these questions as fully as you can:

1. What did you accomplish today? (Include any developments of your project or anything that you learned today.)

____

____

2. What are you, individually, going to do during the next work session?

____

____

3. What are some examples of good teamwork displayed by your team today? (You might include how you solved problems together, what you did when you disagreed, how the team members treated one another, etc.)

____

____

4. What does your team need to improve for next time, and what is your plan of action to make this improvement?

____

____

research based on at least three pieces of literature. Students were to identify at least three different appropriate audiences for their presentation, select one of these, and then design a six-minute presentation, adopting a specific persona that suited that audience. The directions for her assignment follow:

First, you will sit in the student desk to the left side of the classroom. In that desk you will be *you,* explaining to us what you have been creating as your presentation.

1. You will tell us the role you are going to assume as the presenter of this information we are going to hear. *[For example, my name is Linda Hughs, and I am in my first year of studies at Kenyon College, where I am majoring in biology. This past year I was asked to be student director of the Arachnid House at Kenyon College. Today I have come to speak to the Manhasset Chapter of the Arachnid Society.]*

2. Then you will define the audience to which you have planned to give your presentation. (We who are in the audience are supposed to then think like that audience might think.) *[The Arachnid Society is a group of teenagers who are interested in spiders and other creepy, crawly things. This meeting is the first in a series of guest speakers who are discussing the importance of biology in a college education.]*

Figure 5.11
Rubric for the Newspaper Find-a-Job Project

	Expert (4)	Advanced (3)	Novice (2)	Beginner (1)	Uh-Oh (0)
Computation	Error-free	Correct method is chosen, but there is a computation error	Correct method is chosen, but there are two or three computation errors	Incorrect method is chosen, *or* more than three computation errors	Incorrect method is chosen *and* errors in computation
Completeness	Paperwork is complete as per instructions	Labels are missing	Ads are missing	Computations are missing	Ads *and* computations are missing
Organization	Everything is where it belongs	Work goes beyond space allotted	Work from one space interferes with other work	Work is in wrong space	No apparent organization of work
Neatness	Error and correction free	Clear and easy to read	Changes and/or corrections are distracting to reader	Changes and/or corrections interfere with reader's ability to understand answers	Work is illegible
Timeliness	On time	On time, but in locker	Completed during the day it's due and handed in before the end of the day	One day late	More than one day late
Process	Used by teacher to assist other students	Completes own work, without assistance	Completes work, with peer assistance	Completes work, with adult assistance	Doesn't ask for needed help

3. Then you will hint at or tell us the purpose of your presentation. *[My purpose is to tell you about my experience with the spiders I worked with last year and how I became interested in these fascinating creatures.]*

Next, you will go to the place in the classroom where you are going to give your presentation. If you are going to rearrange the room, please tell me the day before so I am prepared to help. You will get into your costume at the beginning of class. Make sure you have your visual aid ready to go (if you are using one).

Your presentation should last about six minutes. (Unfortunately, we are a bit pressed for time, so please be ready to go when it is your turn.)

Finally, after you are finished, you should remove all of your belongings while the next person gets ready to present.

Figure 5.12
Student- and Teacher-Designed Rubric for a 7th Grade Presentation Project

Student ______________________________

Evaluator ______________________________

	Exemplary	Excellent to Great	Good to Needs Improvement	Poor to Unacceptable
Creation of Audience	• Vividly describes the audience • Perfect match between audience and presentation • Audience clearly exists in the real world	• Describes a specific audience • Audience and presentation clearly match • Audience could exist in the real world	• Describes the audience in general or vague terms • Audience and presentation match somewhat • Audience might exist but rarely or it's forced	• Gives no description of the audience • Audience and presentation don't match • No such audience exists in the real world
Role as Presenter	• Plays role flawlessly; an "Academy Award" performance • Audience forgets you are playing a role • Uses authentic costumes and props • Your viewpoint appears inarguable	• Role is believable for the presentation • Stays "in character" throughout the presentation • Costumes and props are appropriate for the role • Is persuasive and accurate	• Little evidence of role • Falls "out of character" occasionally • Costumes/props don't create role adequately • Your viewpoint is somewhat accurate	• No evidence of role • Characterization doesn't exist • Uses no costumes or props • Audience doesn't understand your viewpoint
Content of Presentation and Use of Books	• Presentation is exactly as proposed and completely realistic • Format is meticulously planned • References to books are original • Uses abundant books • Quotes were essential to the structure of the presentation and its message • Perfectly pronounces titles and authors and makes a variety of references to authors	• A clear match between purpose of presentation and actual performance • Format has a clear structure • Integrates references to books into the presentation • Uses three to four titles • Quotes support the points being made; a minimum of three used • Accurately pronounces titles and authors	• Match between purpose of presentation and actual performance is hard to understand • Format lacks organization • Mentions books but doesn't make relationship clear • Mentions fewer than three titles • Quotes have little connection to the presentation's purpose and theme • Weak pronunciation	• No match between stated purpose and the presentation itself • Format is disorganized • Doesn't mention any books and makes no references • Uses only one book • Uses no quotes • Incorrect pronunciation

Note: A podium will be available, as well as a pair of desks that you can use as a table or a large desk. Also, I am planning to videotape some of these presentations and may need some volunteers.

The rubric for this assignment is in Figure 5.12

Figure 5.13 provides an example of a 7th grader's outline of a presentation.

Student Work

As the examples I've presented show, the assessments include measures that guide student

Figure 5.13
A 7th Grader's Outline for a Presentation Project

Describe your audience: parent(s)-to-be
pregnant wives.

What do you want to teach this audience? I want to teach this audience to discipline their child(ren) without physically hurting them. I also want to teach them child abuse is wrong.

What format will you use to teach this audience?
I would use videos to show the affects on the life of an abused child and the severe punishments used to the abuser(s).

What materials will you need?
I would need a T.V. set and a video tape. (A pointer, I guess).

reflection on both products and processes that may take the form of specific questions, checklists, or rubrics. Reflections and prompts show the teacher's understanding of the need to accommodate the various developmental levels and learning styles. The essence of a student portfolio is the student's reflection on his or her work.

The first example is a weekly reflective log that Andrea Gerstenblatt uses with her 2nd graders. Figure 5.14 (pp. 63–65) shows excerpts from student Jeanne's reflections and her teacher's responses. They show how Andrea enhances the student's ability to set and monitor goals for her learning.

The second example, which comes from Linda Hughs' 7th grade class, is Sarah's summary reflection on her presentation to her peers and the class:

> *I certainly learned a lot by creating this presentation. I learned how to act (what I mean is I learned different characteristics of people). I discovered different types of costumes, and I found out how they help to create one's role. For instance, if you are trying to look like a businessman, you don't come in dressed in jeans and a T-shirt. Most businessmen wear suits. I also learned other characteristics of people, such as how they walk. A businessman will usually walk briskly without really stopping to notice anything. To add to this, I learned a little bit about videotaping and making a movie. Writing a script isn't always easy. Also, you have to really get your characters to practice a lot before taping.*
>
> *I found out that people can actually learn things from fictional books. For instance, I discovered that drugs are a result of family conflicts. I was able to make connections between my seven books and found out that one's future with drugs depends on one's past with their family. Most of the characters in the book were badly influenced by their family, but some of them were influenced against drugs. There were also more subtle facts "hidden" in my books. For example, I was reading about drugs and my books included information such as types of drugs and side effects of drugs.*
>
> *In writing the learning log, I learned how to analyze and link books together. Each night as I was reading, I thought about this book in comparison to that book. I recorded these ideas in my log.*
>
> *Another thing I learned in creating this presentation is BE SPECIFIC! I know that if I hadn't described my audience in a lot of detail, they would have no idea what I was talking about. I found out that when some people were describing their books using quotes, I got a strong picture in my mind of what they were trying to teach me.*
>
> *I think the most important thing I learned creating this presentation was that a lot of hard work leads to good satisfaction.*

The final example also comes from Linda Hughs' class and is the letter to the portfolio reader written by one of her students:

> *Dear Reader,*
>
> *My name is Lauriana. This notebook is absolute evidence of everything I did during this research. It bluntly shows my growth and learning. I went from confusion about a topic to complete knowledge and interest in anorexia nervosa in a shocking period of time. The learning I have done thanks to this is outstanding and the time I devoted well spent. I worked very hard on this and am extremely proud. The books I read on anorexia nervosa were compelling and eminently blunt. I had some confusion about my topic at first. I abandoned several books and changed my topic. It really took me a while now that I think about it. I wasted a lot of time! Last year I saw a 20/20 about anorexia and I was really interested! Let me explain the learning log. The learning log was a journal that kept track of the things I did everyday. It basically displays my project emerging slowly but surely. The books I read were easy to find because my mom did that for me. she went to the library and took out four books that I happened to love! The presentation was a major learning experience. I had to*

Figure 5.14
Excerpts from 2nd Grader Jeanne's Weekly Log and Her Teacher's Responses

1–16

This week I Learned To do porfolio werK.

I had trouble with,
① compromising with others.
② Being bossey.
③ Listen to others. (Realy listen not pretending to listen.) ④ Math.

Next week I want to work on, ① compromising with others.
② Being Bossey.
③ Realy listen to others.
④ Study Math.

Dear Jeanne,

You did a great job reflecting on your week. What made you think you had trouble compromising with others? How do you think

Figure 5.14 (Continued)

really listening to others will change things for you? What does listening look like? I know you will work hard to reach your goals! ☺

♡ Miss G.

1-23

Dear Miss G.

Bening Bossey made me Think of compromising with others. And if I Really listen I could lerm a lot. And you will know when I am listening or not because you will see a specil expretion on my face. I don't realy Think I reaced the conpromising part but I tried to not be bossey or a little hog hog! But I reached The Math part because I got 100 and nothing wrong on the math test, so, for a reward my mom made my favorite dinner, shirimp salade sandwichies!

♥ Jeanne ☮

Figure 5.14 ***(Continued)***

Dear Jeanne,

I think you are doing a really wonderful job reflecting on your goals. I'm glad you reached your math goal. You must have studied very hard! As for your other goals, I think if you try to do them in little Steps, you might be more successful. Let me know what that "Special expression" is on your face when you are really listening!

♡ Miss G.

stand up in front of an audience I created and teach them about anorexia. The work was hard but it most definitely paid off.

Sincerely,
Lauriana

To further clarify the use of assessment and reflections, Linda includes samples of student work with clear explanations about how the assessments work with different students. She also describes the degree to which the student's work included in her portfolio captures the diversity of the classroom, allowing the reader to draw conclusions about the value of the assessment for wide ranges in student ability and knowledge.

Making Learning Richer and More Meaningful

The teacher-as-curriculum-and-assessment developer portfolio is a priceless document that showcases the thinking and work invested by teachers as they seek to make learning for students richer and more meaningful. It reveals the essence of teachers' practices and allows those who are outside the classroom to better understand the professional qualities that make teaching and learning possible. Julie Kopp, a 2nd grade teacher in the Penfield School District, in Penfield, New York, is eloquent about the rewards associated with keeping a teacher-as-curriculum-and-assessment developer portfolio. Here is an excerpt from her portfolio:

> This year's portfolio did many things for me:
>
> • It helped me identify the outcomes that are part of creating a literate community and streamlining my curriculum. My program is now more cohesive, with each component building on another one in a well-defined way.
> • The process of creating a research unit allowed me to see the interrelatedness of all aspects of a "good" unit. Outcomes, indicators, rubrics, authentic assessments work together as a whole.
> • I understood the value of collecting students' work to create anchors and exemplars for my students. I was able to use the work I collected last year to show this year's students what I meant by quality work.
> • Most important, keeping a portfolio and participating in this project has given me the language and framework for understanding my classroom practice at a level that I was unable to define prior to the experience. Elements of good curriculum design have existed in my practice for years. I read, go to conferences, and pride myself in my growth as a learner. However, I had an intuitive sense that what I did made sense, but I could not have defended myself if put on the stand the way I do now. While I still have a lot to learn, I have a clear vision of what my classroom practice is and why my approach makes sense.

6 The Role of Inquiry in Professional Portfolios

Each item I select to include in my portfolio creates an internal struggle—cognitive dissonance. Does the item match the learnings I think it should? Through reflection I am able to resolve this issue and to validate my learning and my work.

—*Lauren S. Bolonda, high school teacher*
Canandaigua, New York

Action research is the process of seeking answers to important, meaningful questions about one's classroom, one's school, or other professional practice. We'll look at two types of portfolios in this chapter.

First, a *teacher/administrator-as-researcher portfolio* allows teachers and administrators to systematically document and analyze areas of inquiry. Many authors have addressed the question, Why should teachers conduct inquiry and action research (e.g., Schon, 1983; Elliott, 1991; and Glanz, 1998). It encourages them to develop a rationale for their teaching practices. It helps to clarify unforseen consequences and ramifications of work to be undertaken, and it lets readers become involved in a constructive and participatory manner. Portfolios developed for the purpose of research should include a description of the writer's action research, which includes:

- A rationale for the project.
- A description of the actions being taken and studied.
- Questions that include the actions to be taken and that guide the writer in collecting and analyzing the data.
- A description of the curriculum and assessment efforts that are at the heart of the writer's stated research questions.
- A list of data collection techniques that capture actions taken, circumstances, and results of actions that are realistic and manageable.
- A realistic and manageable time line for collection, analysis, and write up of data.
- New questions that emerge from the research and that provide direction for further study.

Teachers or administrators who have reviewed professional literature or research that relates to their research questions can also include that information in their action research portfolios. Inquiry can occur within or outside the classroom. Non-classroom-based inquiry often includes the work of teachers as professional developers. The field of professional development has been studied extensively over the past few years by several commissions—see, for example, *Teachers Take Charge of Their Learning*, produced by the National Foundation for the Improvement of Education (Rényi, 1996). Reports such as this one underscore the problems inherent in many of the professional development opportunities that are accessible to teachers. Whereas some of these problems are true for administrators, their schedules and multiple responsibilities often preclude them from attending or fully engaging in professional development activities.

- Isolated individual learning.
- Fragmented, one-shot training.
- District-level, one-size-fits-all programs.
- Bureaucratically convenient programs.
- Education outside of the workplace.
- Experts telling teachers what to do.
- Skills that everyone can use and therefore are deeply available to no one.
- Teachers as passive receivers.
- Adult learning as an add-on that's not essential to school.

Although reports and studies vary in their specific prescriptions for improving staff development, they share some suggestions. For example, they

- Seek to improve learning among all students.
- Are rigorous and integrate content and processes.
- Are diversified.
- Are ongoing and sustained.
- Require active engagement of participants.
- Are responsive to individual needs.
- Incorporate reflection and inquiry.
- Are collegial and supportive of learning communities.
- Are job-embedded.
- Are systemic.

Second, we'll examine the *teacher/administrator-as-professional-developer portfolio.* Included in this portfolio are descriptions of activities that build on the person's expertise as he or she seeks to put into action best professional development practices. The professional developer includes descriptions of the targeted levels of experience of the audience; supporting resources used to facilitate learning; and evaluation activities and instruments used to monitor

Figure 6.1
Teacher/Administrator-as-Researcher Rubric for an Exemplary Portfolio*

Overall: The portfolio tells the story of the teacher/administrator-as-researcher in the process of looking for answers to questions that are at the heart of his thinking. The action research extends naturally from the person's work and drives his thinking. The reader gets a clear picture of a teacher/administrator who is always wearing the "hat" of a researcher—observing, noting, and thinking about what happens and why.

Action Research: The teacher's/administrator's assessment work and reflections clearly connect to his stated research questions. The designed research plan is sound, and methods of collection fit snugly into the writer's assessment design. The research is an integral and natural part of his work. The data collected are clearly presented, accurately summarized, and thoroughly analyzed. The reader can only agree with the conclusions drawn, as the evidence provided is compelling. New questions naturally emerge for the research and provide direction for further study. The teacher/administrator is compelled to continue the quest for answers to these new questions and has clearly defined a plan for continued research efforts.

*The entire Teacher/Administrator-as-Researcher Portfolio Rubric appears in Appendix 7 (p. 108).

Figure 6.2
Teacher/Administrator-as-Professional-Developer Rubric for an Exemplary Portfolio*

Overall: The portfolio tells the story of a teacher/administrator who has clearly defined her areas of expertise and who has outstanding ability to share that expertise. By leading workshops, facilitating collegial circles, coaching peers, and writing articles for publication, the teacher/administrator is contributing to the collective knowledge of other educators.

Description of Activities: The teacher's/administrator's portfolio includes thorough descriptions of professional development activities that build on her expertise. The context is described and consistent with the teacher's/administrator's planned activities. The programs accommodate the various levels of experience of the audience and are based on sound learning theory and an understanding of conditions that support adult learning. The presentation serves as a model for good professional development.

Supporting Resources: The materials used by the teacher/administrator are clear, precise, professional, and attractive. The teacher/administrator has consistently sought feedback from participants and included the feedback in her portfolio.

Reflection and Analysis: The teacher/administrator has reflected on her own learning as professional developer and specifically discusses strengths and areas for improvement. She has summarized the feedback and has used it to inform future plans. Finally, the teacher/administrator has set clear, specific goals for further professional development activities and documentation of expertise.

*The entire Teacher/Administrator-as-Professional-Developer Portfolio Rubric appears in Appendix 8 (p. 110).

programs. This portfolio also includes teachers' or administrators' reflections on their own learning as staff developers and discusses strengths, areas for improvement, and strategies for further growth.

In this chapter, I will portray the role of inquiry in the portfolios of teachers/administrators-as-researchers and teachers/administrators-as-professional-developers. Figure 6.1 is a description of what an exemplary portfolio for the former looks like. The entire rubric appears in Appendix 7 (p. 108). Figure 6.2 is a description of what an exemplary teacher/administrator-as-professional-developer portfolio looks like. The entire rubric appears in Appendix 8 (p. 110).

Using the umbrella of inquiry, I will describe the kinds of activities that teachers engage in as they investigate their roles within and outside the classroom. Snapshots of teachers at work will provide glimpses of these activities.

Classroom-Based Inquiry

A 5th Grade Class

Lee Pfister is a 5th grade teacher in the Levittown School District, in Levittown, New York. Lee used action research to explore the role of scoring rubrics in improving student achievement. To provide a context for understanding her analysis of students' work, Lee provided the reader with some background information on the use of rubrics. Her research question was, How will the development and use of rubrics impact students' performance in a composition? To explore this question, she selected and studied the work of three children of different writing abilities. Following are some excerpts from her analysis for two of her students.

> My first encounter with rubrics was when I tried to adapt the New York State Writing Test rubrics so that my students could understand and use

them. After a summer course, I seriously tried to write a rubric with a colleague from my school. The rubric was fine except that students had too much to check at one time. I decided to have them select just three things for them to master during a given writing assignment.

As I got braver, I established a rubric with my class for their mystery book report. Even though I asked for their input, I made sure they incorporated everything I wanted into the rubric. As I've gained confidence, I have let the children produce more rubrics. I have even asked them to advise me on the assignments that they think deserve to be graded with a rubric. When they use a rubric, I ask them to explain their reasoning for their scores.

The preceding background information shows Lee's shift from having exclusive control over the assessment process to having students share control by generating the criteria for a scoring rubric. Fairly quickly, Lee learned how rubrics could help writers at every ability level:

> Eric goes to the resource room. He has trouble spelling and is in a low reading group. He has a tendency not to finish his work. I did not originally plan to include him in my research, but, as I examined his work, I wondered if it was appropriate to use the same rubric with students whose performance is much lower than the rest of the class. After talking to the resource room teacher, we decided to score him the same as everyone else, although we offered him the opportunity to redo his story if he was not happy with his score.
>
> When Eric first came to my class I wasn't sure he would pass the New York State Writing Test. He wrote short, choppy paragraphs. With the use of reflection and rubrics, Eric has changed dramatically. He still has trouble with spelling, but he has developed his own personal style of writing. He struggles to earn a 3 on the rubric, but was able to pass the New York State test. His reflections on his writing show that he has internalized the scoring rubric because he uses the language of the rubric to evaluate his story. At times, he has chosen to revise his work to earn a higher score.
>
> Jessica, a bright child, came into my class as a good writer. One of the things I hoped the rubric would do for her is challenge her to grow. I decided to increase the top score of my rubric to stretch her. While Jessica came to me as a good writer, she was afraid to take chances. Allowing her to use the rubric as a tool was a great help. Once she realized that she could fix problems on the rough draft without being penalized, she started to take risks. Jessica had to work for the top score on the rubric. In her spring portfolio survey she stated that she had "learned to use precise vocabulary, action verbs, similes, and metaphors." She also wrote that she wanted to have a voice and make readers interested in her writing through a good lead. Her explanations demonstrate that she had internalized the rubric.

In addition to analyzing the work of a few students in depth, Lee gathered some data on her class to examine the role of rubrics in supporting learning:

> Children constantly mentioned what we stressed in our rubrics when they discussed their writing. They used the rubrics as tools to improve their writing rather than to discuss their grades. The combination of rubrics with models of writing was powerful. I concluded that rubrics are important in helping students to improve their writing.

7th Grade English Students

Shelley Gentile is a 7th grade English teacher in the Sodus School District, in New York. Shelley decided to explore strategies for fostering students' reflection and for using their feedback to improve upon her practice. As part of her action research inquiry, Shelley asked her students, "How do you feel about our process for writing a descriptive essay?" and "What areas of spelling do you find difficult?"

After listing and analyzing her students' responses to these questions, Shelley learned that, even though students gave more answers to her first question than to the second one, their responses were directed at all aspects of writing or were too ambiguous (Figure 6.3). On the other hand, her second reflective question (Figure 6.4) yielded many specific responses that could help her improve her teaching. The quality of students' responses was directly linked to the specificity of the questions. Her action research portfolio also included a narrative on her history of using reflection with her students, the data she had collected on her students' reflective responses to questions, and her analysis of these data.

High School English Classes

Linda Bohrer is a high school English teacher in the Hilton School District in Hilton, New York. Linda has always been curious about how to best produce good readers. She constantly asks herself, How do students become good readers? What do good readers do? What can teachers do to enable students to become good readers? Over the past few years, Linda has been frustrated with the lack of preparation of entering high school students. The purposes of her action research were to assess incoming 9th grade stu-

Figure 6.3
7th Graders' *General* Reflections on Question #1: How Do You Feel About Our Process for Writing a Descriptive Essay?

Likes	Dislikes
• It was fine. • It was easy to work with. • It was organized and easier. • I like how it gave you the basic idea of the paragraph and you just filled in the details. • I like how you started it off for us and we just finished it. • I liked it because it's organized. • It helped me. • I didn't really like it in any way besides the fact that it was easy. • I liked it because we didn't have to think of everything by ourselves, it was easier. • It was easier than thinking about writing something. • There was nothing I didn't like. • I liked it all because we did it together. • I liked it because you made sure everyone understood. I didn't dislike it. The sheet was very helpful because I knew exactly what I had to write.	• I much prefer writing on my own. • There wasn't enough space. • I didn't like the whole thing. I hate to write. • It took a long time. • Nothing. • I didn't like how there wasn't a lot of space. • I didn't like it, it was too long. • How the first sentence in a paragraph started. • Did not stress creativity. • Too much writing. • I did not like it. • You went too fast.

Figure 6.4
7th Graders' *Specific* Reflections on Question #2:
What Areas of Spelling Do You Find Difficult?

- Remembering all the rules.
- I can't understand the teacher saying the word.
- Vowels.
- Remembering how to spell a word and the word's punctuation.
- Spelling.
- Writing the words too fast, rules, and vowel sounds.
- Remembering all the words.
- I have trouble spelling long words.
- What vowels go where.
- Listening to the words.
- I don't have big problems with spelling.
- Spelling things right.
- Words with silent *e.*
- Everything.
- Words with silent letters.
- Different letters that sound the same.
- Remembering how to spell it and adding things and subtracting things [prefixes and suffixes].
- When I don't study.
- Having to spell a word out loud without being able to write it down.

dents' reading abilities and attitudes toward reading, and to monitor each student's growth in reading. Her action research questions included:

- How will instruction in reading strategies (think aloud and reciprocal reading) impact reading skills?
- How can a reading portfolio document reading achievement and growth?
- Are the assessment tools for monitoring student progress suitable?

Unlike Lee, who used case study research to address her research question, Linda combined weekly logs and curriculum-embedded measures of student achievement as her methodology. Linda recorded the progress of her research. Following are some excerpts from her log:

Week 2

This 4th period class is certainly a wide mix of kids. Not only do I have eight students who are less able, but in the same class I have three students who are extremely bright. How am I going to deal with this? The whole premise of this project is based upon instruction in reading strategies to improve reading skills, and already I can see that these talented students are bored to tears.

Week 3

We began with an introduction to mythology and did some reading about the creation of the world. Many of the lower-ability students refuse to read aloud in class. I'm puzzled—are they just being defiant, or are they ashamed of their lack of ability to read aloud? The more able students volunteer all the time—maybe to speed things along? . . . I need to reassess what I am doing.

In her initial inquiry, Linda sought to examine the role of two different reading strategies on students' achievement, but the realities of her classroom led her to expand her inquiry to address the needs of different learners in her classroom. This is not an uncommon occurrence when doing classroom research. Rather, it is typical for a teacher's research question to change during action research.

> *Week 4*
>
> This week I think I solved the problem of challenging my higher-ability students while continuing to teach reading strategies to the rest of the class. I have developed a number of project ideas for them to pursue while the rest of the class reads and practices strategies. I have made arrangements with the librarian for the students (all girls) to go the library to work on their chosen project I will also give them the material that the rest of the class is reading.
>
> *Week 7*
>
> We read more short myths, and then students were to create their own myths. The results were very good—I was pleasantly surprised by the quality of writing; many were quite imaginative and showed understanding of the purpose of myths. I'm beginning to think that all of our effort is paying off. I have also noted that some of my reluctant readers are volunteering more to share during the think-alouds and reciprocal reading.

A 2nd Grader with Behavioral Problems

Teacher inquiry varies greatly. Whereas some research focuses on the impact of certain strategies or curriculum on learning, other research is prompted by the need to understand the possibilities and limitations of teachers in producing learning and other effects. Patricia Lynch is a 2nd grade teacher in the Manhasset Public Schools in Manhasset, New York. Her inquiry was prompted by frustration over her inability to help one of her students. This student displayed serious behavioral problems that appeared to be linked to emotional issues. Pat sought to understand what she could and could not do under difficult circumstances.

Pat has increasingly wondered about the role of emotional intelligence in a student's learning. Her research involved documenting and analyzing work conducted with a specific student in her class whose disruptive behavior clearly set her apart from the other students. The following narrative from Pat's portfolio invites the reader to enter her classroom and understand her relationship with this student. It is also a lesson in how the most careful and well-intentioned plan can be interrupted when parents are not part of the process or do not believe in the plan.

> Amy is an active 7-year-old. She physically resembles the Olympic Gold Medal winner Tara Lipinsky and shares a passion for ice-skating. She has a younger brother and sister. Amy's mannerisms sometimes seem beyond her years, manipulative and precocious, adolescent in effect. Other times they are parentlike. Her mood and tone of voice can shift from disarmingly charming and coy to hostile and threatening in a moment. She likes to be in charge. She frequently refers to herself as a "bad girl." She is happy, outgoing, and loquacious; sullen and stubborn; disobedient and domineering; quiet, angry, and depressed. Her range of emotions and moods is greater than that of any other child in the class. She is a complex and capable child.
>
> This cauldron of emotions in which Amy stewed was evaporating much of her potential academic achievement. I instinctively knew that this was a bright child whose emotional storms were blocking her learning. There was no inherent cognitive reason why this child should have qualified, as she had, for remedial language arts support since 1st grade.
>
> I had specific goals in mind for Amy. I hoped that she would become more considerate of others, share and be less controlling in a group, reduce her use of hostile facial expressions, soften the tone of her voice, and reduce her use of negative self-talk. All of this would help Amy make friends and improve her ability to learn.

In class, I expected Amy to follow classroom rules. She had the most difficulty during group work. Time-outs were consequences for those times when Amy was disruptive. My strategy was to provide structure by having consistent consequences and to have Amy monitor her own behavior. I also wanted Amy to know that I cared about her as a person. We would talk about the distinction between those behaviors she could improve and her notion of herself as a "bad girl."

In addition to defining specific goals for Amy and developing a plan for helping this child become better socialized in the class, Pat recommended in-school and outside counseling. Only the former was used. Even though Amy's behavior began to improve modestly as soon as counseling began, the research on Amy was abruptly interrupted when her parents pulled her from Pat's class. Pat continues to believe that emotional intelligence plays a serious role in students' learning and is now designing new ways of exploring this issue.

Inquiry Outside the Classroom

Inquiry can occur within the confines of teachers' and administrators' classrooms and schools or as they seek to make changes or affect the thinking or work of other adults.

How Is Adult Learning Different from Students' Learning?

Lisa Boerum is a middle school special education teacher in the Sag Harbor School District in Sag Harbor, New York. Lisa has actively participated in several of the multi-year professional development programs that I have led. While she continues to work full-time as a teacher, Lisa has embraced action research not only as a way to improve her students' learning but also to improve her growing role as a professional developer in her school district. Lisa demonstrates that the real learning for teachers who use action research comes when making sense of the information collected as she writes and explains to herself the questions she is posing and the answers she is gleaning from her inquiry.

Lisa's research question was: "What are some differences and similarities between adults and children in terms of their learning needs?" Lisa's ability to use self-reflection and inquiry to understand teaching and learning is evident in the following portfolio reflection. She wrote it during one of the assessment courses she has taught in her school district.

We are midway through the Assessment Design course, and I am feeling good about the progress of the participants. The first day was setting the stage: laying out the plan and roles we would each play. Showing the assessment and curriculum rubrics at the end of the day left everyone burned out and a little overwhelmed. We didn't read the rubrics all the way through. I just read over some of the dimensions used. By Tuesday we had charted several pages of questions and comments on curriculum, pilot tests, exit outcomes, Sag Harbor, and so on. By Tuesday afternoon, standards, indicators, and essential questions threw many of the nine participants into a tizzy.

Amazingly, I remained calm as the conflict erupted and the blaming of all kinds of school personnel and outside agencies began. Everyone reacted in ways so familiar to me: resistance with and without rage, helplessness, fear, and trepidation. I lived through 10 years of at-risk students, and long-term professional development programs. For example, in the Long Island Performance Assessment Project, I saw my students and colleagues experience the same emotions. This has helped me to calmly support my colleagues through their toughest moments.

Lisa's reflection underscores that all learners, whether teachers or students, share similar characteristics, foremost among them a fear of change and the insecurities resulting from grappling with new material. The next excerpt shows the inherent tension between following a teaching plan and responding to the apparent needs of our learners:

> Maybe I should have broken up the first two days and extended them: one day for authenticity and another full day for assessment design. Yet how would they have time to work if I spoke so much? I guess I assumed that they had the tools for self-discovery when what they may have needed was a more guided tour. I was able, after the storm, to individually show those who needed it, point-by-point, the process I went through in writing my own assessments.

In her reflection, Lisa shows the needed restraint that teachers ought to exercise when they know that letting students grapple with ambiguity, complexity, or uncertainty is more valuable than the short-term satisfaction of having an answer:

> I can see that they wanted so much to find out what I wanted—what the right answer was. Slowly, through the end of Tuesday and into Wednesday, they became more independent. . . .
>
> I realize that there is no real difference between us and our students in the way we move through a new experience. If we, as facilitators of learning, allow students to explore, they will . . . blindly at first. But if we give them guidance on where to look and what to look for, they will discover. If we validate their frustrations and maintain our expectations, they will rise to meet them. If we support and encourage them through the most trying moments, they will begin to realize their strengths. If we live as if learning is a journey on which to pursue the essence of quality, they will see their learning as a journey, travel with us for a while, and participate more actively in the pursuit of quality than they had before.

Lisa's ongoing inquiry allowed her to monitor the merits and shortcomings of her materials:

> One of the most useful handouts was my inverted triangle, which structured Essential Topic, Rationale, and Skill Focus from a broad to narrow scope. I also gave them an additional way of looking at the components of the design that they were responsible for providing at the end of the course. I found that these teachers were, for the most part, linear thinkers and it was easier for them to focus on broad to narrow.

As is often the case, action research leads to new questions, goals, and research activities:

> Next time I would like to develop a working packet for the design, where each step is on a different page with an explanation for what to think about and what to produce. I think that this would alleviate the stress of not seeing the big picture. It wasn't as if I didn't present the big picture to them in several ways. I did. They just didn't see it. They saw only the piece they were up to, and they kept thinking they were done, not realizing there was more to do. My thought was so typical of teachers: If they had read the overview when I told them to, they would know. I realize, as with our students, that you have to keep telling them in different ways—whole to part to whole, so they don't get caught off guard.

Lisa's action research within her professional developer portfolio is a living testament of her triumphs:

> Today I recall a significant moment for several teachers on the Thursday of the workshop. The

independent work atmosphere sustained itself to the point where I was looking for people to conference with as opposed to their waiting for me. One teacher, Jim, a very hard worker who teaches 11th grade social studies, began to see the vision. When he asked me about the difference between a rationale and an overview, I took out the introduction packet to this course and read to him my rationale and overview for the course. "Wow" was somewhat like his response.

A little later on, he had me read his version for the unit he was developing on the Articles of Confederation and the Constitution. Jim had a commendable draft of a rationale that addresses the global issue of a citizen's responsibility toward awareness of and participation in the events of the governments around him.

I truly felt that I have grown this week as well. I allowed myself to be vulnerable enough to facilitate these teachers through a demanding process. They respected me enough to stay, when by Tuesday they really wanted to leave. They went through many of the emotions they themselves listed as characteristics of authentic learning, and lived to tell about it. They incorporated in their design a plan for implementing some of the items they themselves listed as best teacher strategies on the first day of the class. They have come full circle for now, and so have I. . . .

English Teachers Develop Authentic Assessments

Liz Galdi-Locatelli is an English teacher in North Rockland Central School District in New York. She has developed a number of different strategies to assist district teachers in developing authentic assessments.

One such strategy involves giving teachers contrasting tasks that address the same learning outcomes. Liz asks them to identify the differences between the parallel tasks, to create their own definition of authentic tasks, and to ponder the question: Is content sacrificed as tasks become more authentic? She does this by showing them pairs of tasks that address the same learning outcomes. One of the tasks is a traditional learning and assessment task, whereas the other is a complete and contextualized task that is directed to a plausible or authentic audience and/or that addresses a purpose students recognize as important outside of school. Figure 6.5 is a comparison of traditional and authentic tasks.

For example, one of her tasks asks students to identify the author and the work from which some quotes are excerpted. The authentic task in this pair asks students to assume they are taking a trip in a time machine that will allow them to visit famous classical authors. During their visits, students will talk with one of those authors about his philosophy and exchange opinions. Then they record their visits in the form of an annotated script and a letter exchange.

Action research can be as helpful to administrators as it is to teachers. Often this form of inquiry allows administrators to make sense of new roles and to exercise democratic forms of instructional leadership. The portfolio of Kathleen Fuller, a former assistant principal at Hilton High School in Hilton, New York, is a case in point.

In her first year in this role, Kathleen was concerned about how to help teachers self-monitor and improve. She had just participated in her district's three-year professional development program on authentic assessment and learner-centered education. As an assistant principal, Kathleen focused her action research on developing a teacher self-evaluation process that incorporated much of what she had learned in this program. She developed a rubric to help teachers develop their own self-evaluation projects. Because she developed this rubric with teachers, it underscored the value of rubrics as instructional and assessment tools, and allowed

Figure 6.5
A Comparison of Traditional and Authentic Tasks

Traditional Tasks

Task: Mark Twain lives in American letters as a great artist, the writer whom William Dean Howells called "the Lincoln of our Literature."

Agree or disagree with this statement, using Twain's portrayal of Jim as evidence of his attitudes toward the slavery issue. Write a character analysis to support your position. Include examples of Jim's behavior as well as statements made by Jim and about him.

Task: You have been given a list of quotes from Emerson, Thoreau, and Bryant. For each quote, identify the author and the work. Then explain the meaning of the passage in your own words.

Select one of the quotes, and write a personal reaction to its message.

Desired Outcomes:

1. Locate and access biographical and critical information on a given author.
2. Maintain integrity of source in selecting and using information.

Task: Select one of the listed American authors. Write a research paper of three to five typed pages. Your paper must include a discussion of each of the following:

- Biography (include only important details).
- Influences on his works.
- Writer's place in American literature (include comments by literary critics).
- Influence on other writers, if applicable.
- List of major works and themes.

Authentic Tasks

Task: *The Adventures of Huckleberry Finn* is taught in the 10th grade at your school. Recently, some parents approach the school board, objecting to the teaching of this novel. Claiming the book presents a negative view of blacks, they cite the use of the term *nigger,* the use of dialect, and the characterization of Jim as evidence.

As a student who has studied this novel, you have been asked to present your views to the board. Because some adults present may not be familiar with the book, you are to be prepared to cite specific examples and passages to defend your position.

Task: You have the opportunity to take a trip in a time machine. Use this opportunity to visit either Emerson, Bryant, or Thoreau. During your visit, ask questions, discuss transcendental philosophy, and express your own opinions. To share your experience with others, you may choose to

- Record your entire conversation, presenting both sides of the discussion.
- Record parts of your conversation, and add a commentary on the author's surroundings, attitude, and responses.
- Present letters written between you and the author during your visit to the past.

Desired Outcomes:

1. Locate and access biographical and critical information on a given author.
2. Maintain integrity of source in selecting and using information.
3. Synthesize information to present a fresh, personal perspective.

Task: In keeping with the "less is more" philosophy of education, the English Department in your school has decided to select a limited number of American authors to be studied in depth. Your teacher has asked for your input.

Prepare to convince your teacher that the author you are recommending should be included on the list. In your presentation be sure to give reasons your teacher can accept, and to support your reasons with specific information about the author and his or her works. Keep in mind that the more knowledgeable you seem, the more seriously your recommendation will be taken.

(continues on next page)

Figure 6.5 (continued)

Task: Read the short story "Regret" by Kate Chopin. Then write an essay to show that this story belongs in the section on Realism in your anthology. To do this, you will need to identify characteristics of Realism and cite examples from the story to show that it represents this literary period.	***Task:*** Your school's literary magazine is preparing an exposé on life in Rockland County, and you have been asked to make a contribution. To prepare, brainstorm situations in your everyday life at home or at school that can be used to reflect your lifestyle. After you have selected the most interesting situation, select one moment that conveys a significant concept about human nature or human relationships. Then write a brief but concrete piece to communicate clearly the truth you wish to express. You can borrow effective writing techniques from authors you have studied in the Realism section of your text. These techniques include concrete details, sensory images, irony, sarcasm, metaphors, similes, vivid verbs, and dialect.
Desired Outcomes: Students can identify characteristics of literature from the Realism period and can explain how a given piece fits this literary style.	***Desired Outcomes:*** Students can identify the characteristics of literature from the Realism period and apply what they have learned from literature to help them to present a critical view of their own society.

Kathleen to study the process of developing rubrics with teachers:

> I invited all teachers participating in the self-directed evaluation plans to help create this rubric using the information the district sets forth about this process. As we began to discuss the rubric, we focused on the obvious components of the plan: goals and actions. I was concerned about the depth of content or plans, while teachers mainly focused on content.
>
> After developing the first draft of the rubric, I began to have conferences with teachers about their proposed plans. As those conferences evolved with the use of the rubric, I saw that the plan should ultimately result in an impact on student performance. This was an element missing from the rubric. As teachers were available, I asked them to meet to discuss revising the rubric to add a category for student performance. Also, as part of my conferences with teachers, we evaluate the rubric for effectiveness in guiding teachers during plan development. . . .
>
> The strengths of this rubric are that it provided a focus and clarity to the expectations for teacher self-directed plans. It removed the subjectivity of administrative approval by setting clear expectations while still providing for the open-endedness that teachers need to design a plan that fits their individual learning needs.
>
> I have learned that rubrics never seem to stop needing revision. Each one I have worked on continues to evolve as it is used. Rubrics are a rich source to guide conversations and promote common understanding among those who use them. The resulting information easily provides goals that can be turned around to influence instruction. The caution I have about this process, and at this point it may be too soon to evaluate, is that the user of the rubric may become so focused on the descriptors of the rubric that other important behaviors or goals

are overlooked. The constant revision and evolving of the rubrics and reassessment as they are used make the process reflective and encourage constant rethinking.

Combining action research with the administrative function of evaluating teachers' performance allowed Kathleen to grow further as a learner. Knowing that action research is a never-ending inquiry that often results in more questions than answers enabled her to use every opportunity to refine the rubric as a testimony to everyone's learning rather than as an obstacle to getting the job done.

Inquiry and Professional Portfolios

Inquiry and professional portfolios go hand-in-hand. Inquiry is the means by which teachers and administrators make sense of the complexities of their roles. Professional portfolios become the documents that legitimize and consolidate that inquiry. There is no one right method, but the commonalities are the documentation of facts and feelings, the recording of failures and successes, and the communication of outcomes—more often growth and improvement than not.

7 Practical Strategies for Getting Started

According to Webster's dictionary, the prefix "meta" means change, more comprehensive or transcending. When added to the name of a discipline, it designates a new, related discipline designed to deal critically with the original. I think we could say that teacher portfolios and the reflections within them are meta-teaching. They comprise a new discipline designed to deal critically with the original one. Furthermore, you cannot keep a portfolio and not change. Teacher portfolios cause you to think critically about your work and focus on improving it.

—Lee Foster, middle school teacher
Seneca Falls, New York

Creating professional collections of work is a foreign experience for most teachers and administrators. Even when the idea makes sense, it is often difficult to decide on a starting point. After reading over 500 professional portfolios, I have learned that most portfolios follow one of four different organizational frameworks. I often share these frameworks with teachers and administrators who are in the process of creating their first professional portfolio.

Four Frameworks for Portfolios

The four frameworks address different ways in which a professional can think of himself or herself.

1. *One's organizational role.* The roles that a professional has or plays in the organization is one framework. For example, a teacher or administrator may organize a portfolio around several chapters or sections, each one depicting a different professional role. Examples are the teacher as a learner, assessor, curriculum developer, action researcher, professional developer, or collaborative team member.

2. *A narrative approach.* The teacher or administrator might also frame the portfolio around specific story elements and tell the story of his or her learning. The teacher or administrator is the main character, and the elements described include the setting (school), theme (central issue or idea pursued), and plot (events that unfold throughout the story).

3. *A comparative approach.* In another framework, the teacher or administrator organizes the portfolio in three sections: the past (where he or she was prior to beginning the learning or portfolio work), the present (where the person is in his or her learning or portfolio development), and the future (the goals and strategies for future learning or portfolio work).

4. *Professional goals.* A fourth framework revolves around the goals that the teacher or administrator has set as a professional. Within this framework, the portfolio developer can address questions such as: What are my goals? What goals has my organization identified for

me? What goals have I worked toward? What evidence do I have of growth in each of my goal areas? What evidence do I have of achievement?

Whereas teachers and administrators often choose to work within one of these frameworks, it is not uncommon for them to combine one or more of them. A typical combination involves organizing the portfolio around roles and describing these roles from a comparative perspective

Distinguishing Portfolios by Their Purpose

As with student portfolios, one can conceive of professional portfolios as serving different needs for different audiences. They can be used for internal purposes, such as the developer using the portfolio to set goals, reflect upon and evaluate practices, and safely record questions and concerns. Portfolios can also be used as external devices, such as for professional development and evaluation. One use is no better than the other. However, teachers and administrators run into difficulties when portfolios uses and audiences are confused. It is important to know from the outset whether the portfolio is public or private—and, if public, just who the audience is.

Implementing professional portfolios need not be a massive undertaking, nor does it have to be threatening. Having professionals study their practice by collecting and analyzing their work is a good idea that is likely to be embraced if professionals receive the necessary time and support to try out the idea and make it part of their thinking. For example, invite groups of teachers or administrators to get together and work as a collegial group, first reading and studying the idea of professional portfolios, and then giving themselves some time for field trials. I recommend that such trials go on for at least two years before raising the stakes for the use of professional portfolios or mandating their use.

Making Portfolios Powerful Tools for Learning

Even though I have described the use of portfolios as potential tools for external evaluation elsewhere in this book, I'd like to underscore that the power of a portfolio lies in its potential to legitimize, produce, and maximize learning. There is no better way for teachers or administrators to keep track of their questions, goals, and strategies for improving what they do. Witnessing the conversation between two teachers who are sharing their portfolios can be a great privilege, because there are so few public forums for teachers to exhibit their professionalism.

There are several strategies for helping teachers and administrators use portfolios to maximize their learning.

1. Allow them to generate or at least help identify the assessment criteria to be used in their portfolios. In my own work, I have learned that teachers and administrators can actively decide what they should include in their portfolios, how this work should be reviewed, and how the review process should unfold. The more I trust this idea, the more thoughtfulness I encounter in the portfolios that I read.

Ironically, giving people the freedom to decide what to do with their portfolios is very uncomfortable at first. When I introduce teachers and administrators to portfolios, they are anxious about the open-endedness of my invitation for them to construct and annotate their learning. Some of them insist that I share my own expectations and wishes for their portfolios. It takes time for us to develop the necessary trust for them to own the responsibility of constructing their own personal portfolios without feeling inadequate. Yet the payoff that results from not yielding to giving portfolio developers much structure or requirements is worth working toward.

2. *Provide them with time to work on their portfolios.* It takes time for teachers and administrators to define what they want their portfolios to show about themselves, to compile the appropriate evidence, and to ponder and write about the portfolio's meaning. This is especially important when we consider that teaching and leading are primarily oral performances, rather than written ones. Teachers and administrators are not in the habit of, nor are they expected to articulate their thinking or their work, other than through cryptic lesson plans and memos. In many ways, developing a portfolio is unnatural, at least at this time. Therefore, we must stretch the limits of the culture in which teachers and administrators work and create the conditions that can foster the documentation of teacher expertise and reflective practice. When we build real spaces for educators to think into their daily or weekly routines, we acknowledge the value of thoughtfulness in professional practice.

The principal reason for my being able to review professional portfolios at the end of each school year is that I devote significant blocks of time in the summer and during the school year for teachers and administrators to design, organize, and annotate their portfolios, as well as reflect on their learning.

3. *Inform them of the audience and purpose for their portfolios.* Whereas professional portfolios can be shared with several audiences and used for different purposes, teachers and administrators may be uncomfortable sharing their portfolios unless the audience and the purpose for doing so is clear to everyone. As with student portfolios, even though one of the most important uses of portfolios is to show students' effort and growth, students may feel conflicted about including work in their portfolios that is not their best if they think that their parents might misunderstand it. Similarly, teachers might feel hesitant to show lessons or assessments that are not perfect in their eyes, if they think that peers or their supervisors could use this information against them. Therefore, it is critical that portfolio audiences have identical frames of reference when the portfolios are shared.

4. *Provide educators with a caring audience who can thoughtfully review and respond to their portfolios.* Portfolios can trigger the most wonderful conversations. A well-organized portfolio around clear and explicit outcomes can tell a far richer story about a teacher or an administrator than a conversation or a work-site visit. To the extent that we consider learning to be an ongoing process, we must provide portfolio developers with access to constructive, rigorous feedback on their work and their thinking.

How can we maximize the interchange between portfolio developer and portfolio reviewer? One strategy is modeled after the use of "warm" and "cool" feedback used by the Coalition of Essential Schools. This strategy involves having the portfolio reviewer spend 5 to 10 minutes providing the portfolio developer with warm feedback. This feedback is devoid of traditional praise. Rather, it includes statements of appreciation for the work reviewed; for example:

- The way you organized and annotated your table of contents helped me decide how I would prioritize my reading of your portfolio.
- I can see how I could develop a rubric with my students by looking at your student-developed rubrics and your reflections on them.
- I was able to follow your thinking as you described the curriculum unit you included.

Once the reviewer has no more warm feedback to give, he or she moves to cool feedback. Such feedback includes questions and concerns that are grounded in the portfolio. Some examples follow:

- I was not able to follow how you got from the learner outcomes to the authentic assessment.
- I do not understand what you mean by *thoughtful* when you use that word on the third level of your rubric.
- Why did you decide to include samples of those three students?

This review process works well in small groups where a portfolio developer receives feedback from at least two other people. As a professional developer, I use this technique when teachers and administrators think they are ready to shift from a working portfolio to a showcase or shareable one. Along with the feedback, we ought to create a milieu that encourages educators to revise and improve upon their practice.

5. *Treat portfolios as works in progress.* It is much easier for teachers and administrators to display risk-taking behaviors when they know that they will have future opportunities to revise their work. In this context, it is important to remember that teachers often have unreasonably high expectations for what they can accomplish and in what period of time. Perhaps this is because they are often expected to tackle several innovations at once even though support for implementing them is often lacking. In any case, the systematic inclusion of artifacts, as well as goal-setting and reflection activities that occur in the keeping of professional portfolios, can help teachers and administrators set reasonable goals and develop a sharp focus for their learning.

The Wisdom of Practice

Professional portfolios are a "luxury" because they can be created only when there are opportunities for thoughtfulness. As I conjure images of all the schools and teachers I have worked with, I cannot remember too many opportunities for thoughtfulness. Instead, I visualize fast-paced incidents, unexpected daily crises, frustration, elation, and unexciting drill. We tend to act too fast to think. This frenzied feeling is compounded when we consider that many teachers and administrators are preoccupied with meeting their students' basic needs (like having enough food to feed pupils, or having access to books of any kind). In such instances, it is hard to imagine many opportunities for reflection.

I believe that it is possible to be a reasonably good teacher and not have many opportunities for reflection. Teaching is, after all, as much an art and a product of intuitive thinking as it is a technical craft and professional endeavor. In fact, I have witnessed the work of extraordinary teachers who experience great difficulties articulating their thinking and work, but these are very rare individuals.

Thoughtfulness and the practice of articulating one's thinking in writing aids practice. It allows teachers and administrators to evaluate and improve their work. Portfolios are a powerful means for the articulation of thoughtful practice. They are the repositories of experience, and the bank in which we can deposit the wisdom of practice.

In this book, I have not said everything that ought to be said about professional portfolios. I have merely articulated several approaches to their creation. I am sure that many more approaches are possible and perhaps desirable. I hope that this book will provide readers with sufficient images of thoughtful practice to inspire more widespread use of professional portfolios. I am absolutely convinced that every professional who uses portfolios in a serious way will become a better teacher or administrator.

Appendix I

Hudson Valley Portfolio Assessment Project Checklist for the Review of Teacher-as-Assessor Portfolio

Portfolio developer: ___________________________
Portfolio reviewer: ___________________________
Grade level in which the
portfolio is being used: ___________________
Date: ___________________________________

Please use the following key to determine the extent to which the portfolio in question addresses the criteria listed below:

Not at all 1 2 3 4 5 Definitively

Outcomes and indicators:

____ The portfolio includes learning outcomes to be addressed.
____ The portfolio includes outcome indicators (what the outcomes mean to the teacher).
____ The reader clearly understands what the outcomes and indicators mean.
____ The portfolio describes the relationship among outcomes, indicators, and entries.
____ The reader clearly understands the relationship among outcomes, indicators, and entries included.

Standards and criteria:

____ The portfolio establishes clear criteria for the selection of the entries.
____ If the portfolio is achievement related, it includes appropriate performance standards for judging the quality of the entries.
____ The portfolio clearly distinguishes standards from expectations.
____ If the portfolio is achievement related, it is evaluated.
____ If the portfolio is achievement related, it includes the rubrics used to assess entries.
____ If the portfolio is graded, the reader knows what criteria are used to assess the entries and/or the portfolio as a whole.

Portfolio use:

____ The portfolio clearly describes the time frame that it comprises.
____ The portfolio clearly describes the curriculum areas it addresses.
____ The reader knows the grade level for which the portfolio is designed.
____ The portfolio includes a thorough description of the kinds of students in the class(es) in which it is used.
____ It is evident that the reader knows who the primary audience for the portfolio is.
____ It is evident that the reader knows who the secondary audience(s) for the portfolio is/are.
____ It is evident that the reader knows who owns the portfolio.
____ It is evident that the reader knows what happens to the portfolio when it is completed.

Scope of portfolio:

____ The portfolio appropriately documents students' achievement.

____ The portfolio appropriately documents students' effort.

____ The portfolio appropriately documents students' progress.

Portfolio entries:

____ The reader understands the context surrounding each of the entries (i.e., coached, homework assignment, individual versus group work, etc.).

____ The assignments that produce the portfolio entries are described with sufficient detail.

____ The assignments that produce the portfolio entries are substantive.

____ The portfolio entries are intrinsically connected to the outcomes and indicators.

____ The portfolio clearly describes the role that the teacher, students, and/or others had in selecting the portfolio entries.

____ The portfolio allows for sufficient choice and individualization by students.

____ The portfolio entries adequately assess authentic learning.

____ The portfolio entries are likely to sufficiently reveal students' thinking.

____ The portfolio entries are likely to sufficiently reveal students' development.

____ The portfolio entries require that the student reflect upon them.

____ The portfolio entries are likely to enable students from all cultural backgrounds to demonstrate their knowledge and skills.

Journal (and/or introductory letter to the reader):

____ The journal clarifies the teacher's decision making about what to include in the portfolio.

____ The journal includes sufficient evidence of the steps taken to create and refine the portfolio.

____ The journal includes sufficient information on students' reactions to the portfolio and the required entries.

____ The journal includes sufficient information on the demands, in terms of time and effort, imposed by the use of the portfolio and other alternative assessments.

____ The journal includes sufficient information on the extent to which the portfolio adequately captures the teachers' desired student outcomes.

____ The journal includes sufficient information on the teacher's current assessment of the portfolio.

____ The journal includes sufficient information on the research question that the teacher is pursuing.

1. Overall, what are the strengths of this portfolio?
2. What are its most obvious weaknesses?
3. What are some practical suggestions for addressing these weaknesses?
4. What insights have you derived as a portfolio developer from the review process?
5. What implications does your review of this portfolio have for your own portfolio design?

Response to Peer Review and Self-Assessment

Portfolio developer: ______________________

1. What are the key insights you derived from your reviewer's interpretation of your portfolio?
2. What will you do to this portfolio to improve upon it?

Appendix 2

Hendrick Hudson School District Portfolio Initiative Guidelines

The purpose of the **Teacher-as-Learner Portfolio** that you keep during this program is to document your thinking and learning about assessment

Your task is to put together a portfolio that SHOWS your achievement of the program outcomes, TELLS the story of your learning, and REVEALS you as a reflective learner/teacher/assessor. As you tell the story of your learning, you should focus on the development of the **main character** (you) and provide, for your audiences, the other elements that make a good story, such as **setting, theme, plot,** and **conflict.** Remember that your audiences are yourself, your peers (inside and outside of the project), and your facilitator or coach.

Following are three categories of entries that will guide you in creating a portfolio that contains the elements your reader needs to understand your story. You will choose the specific pieces to put into your portfolio, and you will determine the structure/organization that will most enhance your story for the reader.

Context

The following types of entries can help to describe the **setting** for the story and may serve to further develop the main character of the story. While these may not directly demonstrate your achievement of the course outcomes, they are necessary for your reader to understand your story.

1. A description of your teaching situation: grade, subjects, individual/team teaching.
2. A description of the range and types of students in your class.
3. A curriculum map that identifies the concepts, themes, skills, learning opportunities, and assessments in one, some, or all curricular areas that you teach.
4. The standards that you have for your students with indicators and learning opportunities for each.
5. Descriptions of methods/approaches you use most often in your classroom (e.g., writing workshop, unit approach, inquiry/research focus, interdisciplinary approach to texts) that relate to the work that will be found in your students' portfolios.

Reflections

The following types of reflections can provide insight into the **main character** of the story.

Combinations of them will more fully develop the main character and will reveal the **conflicts** and **themes** in a teacher's story.

1. A Dear Reader letter that guides the reader through the portfolio and tells the story of its development.
2. The teacher's analysis of other strengths as an assessor and areas for improvement, as well as goals and plans for further learning.
3. A philosophy statement describing what the teacher values and believes in.
4. Selected journal entries that reveal the teacher's learning, insights, and struggles about the course content with commentary/analysis.
5. Reflections on/analyses of particular tasks, assessments, and products related to portfolio and authentic assessment.

Portfolio Design and Related Assessments

The following types of entries show what the main character did or created, the **events** that took place during the project that caused him or her to think, learn, and struggle. These can be included in the final form or with all drafts. When included with drafts, the reader is able to see more of the teacher's thinking and learning. Often, **conflicts** and **themes** are revealed and further developed.

1. A description of the portfolio design that includes
   a. The purpose of the portfolio and the intended audience(s).
   b. The outcomes the portfolio is intended to document.
   c. The selection process that students and teachers use.
   d. The ways in which students reflect on the products and processes connected to the portfolio, as well as the portfolio as a whole.
   e. Complete or near-complete student portfolios.
2. Descriptions of tasks/assignments that the teacher created/revised and that students may draw from for portfolio selections. The descriptions include
   a. Explanation of activities that precede, lead, and follow the task/assignment.
   b. The standard(s) that the task/assignment is intended to target.
   c. The criteria used to evaluate the product or process and a description of the ways in which the criteria are developed and used by teacher and students.
   d. Samples of student work that show the reader what the task/assignment looks like in the classroom.
3. Assessment tools that the teacher/students have created, such as criteria, checklists, rubrics, and reflection prompts that are accompanied by a description of the task and by representative student work.

The following questions may help you as you assemble your portfolio. You are not expected to answer all of these questions—choose from them as needed.

Some questions to guide *selections* for the teacher portfolio:

What pieces of my work demonstrate my achievement of the outcomes for the program? How does each piece demonstrate my achievement?

What pieces of my work reveal the conflicts and/or themes that are prevalent in my story as a learner this year? How are they revealed?

What pieces reveal my ability to reflect on my learning, my teaching, and my assessment practices? How do they reveal this?

Some questions to guide the inclusion of *contextual information*:

What standards do I value most for my students? What do I want my students to know or be able to do when they leave my classroom?

What does achievement of the standards look like at my grade level?

What learning opportunities do I provide that target these outcomes?

How does the portfolio fit into what I do in my classroom?

How does my teaching style facilitate or get in the way of using portfolio assessment?

Some questions to guide *reflection*:

What kind of learner am I? What parts of the project have helped me learn most about assessment?

What goals have I set for myself for assessment and/or reflection in my classroom? Why have I set these goals?

What do I understand about assessment or using student portfolios? What is working? What successes am I having?

What am I confused about/struggling with concerning assessment or the use of student portfolios? What questions do I have?

What do I understand about the role of reflection in assessment or portfolio assessment? What questions do I have?

How are students reacting/interacting with their portfolios? What can they do well? What struggles are they having? How can I address their struggles?

What have I struggled most with this year related to assessment or portfolio assessment? Why?

Some questions to guide the *description of the student portfolio design*:

What is the purpose of the student portfolio?

Who will view/use the portfolio? Student? Teacher? Parents? Future teachers?

What do I want the student portfolio to document?

Who will make the selections for the portfolio? How will selections be made? How often will selections be made?

How has student reflection been incorporated into the portfolio? How are students reflecting on products? On processes? On the portfolio?

How does the portfolio fit into my classroom?

How am I managing the portfolio in my classroom?

Some questions to guide the *description of tasks/assignments* that contribute to the student portfolios:

What standard(s) does the assessment target?

What activities precede the assessment?

How are students guided during the assessment?

What are the evaluation criteria, and how were they developed?

How are the evaluation criteria used by teacher and students?

How does the assessment translate in the classroom? What works well? What improvements can be made?

What does the range of student performance look like for this assessment? Which pieces of student work can I include that show the range?

Some questions to guide the *organization* of the portfolio:

What are the possible ways of organizing my portfolio? What is the best structure, sequence, or format for revealing my story?

How can I make the connections between the pieces in the portfolio clear to my reader?

What organization will enhance the main character, themes, and conflicts of my story?

Appendix 3

Hendrick Hudson Teacher/Administrator-as-Learner Portfolio Rubric

	• The writer is clearly aware of the audience. There is a clear and thorough description of the context within which the work and learning have taken place. • There is a thorough and detailed description of – the community and district, – the school, – the writer's position and responsibilities, – the class/teacher population, – the curriculum/program, – current school and/or district initiatives, – the writer's educational background and history in the field.	• The writer is aware of the audience. There is a clear description of the context within which the work and learning have taken place. • There is detailed description of – the community and district, – the school, – the writer's position and responsibilities, – the class/teacher population, – the curriculum/program.	• The writer writes more for herself or himself than the audience. The reader must read between the lines and guess at the context for the work and learning described. • There is general description of – the writer's position, – the curriculum/program.	• The writer has forgotten that there is an audience. The context for the work and learning needs to be described. • There is mention of grade level and/or subject area or general work responsibilities.	
	• The portfolio reveals substantial evidence of thoughtfulness and reflectivity. • The writer's reflections – reveal new insights on course content and application of new concepts, – reveal concerns with course content and application of new concepts, – include questions for further inquiry, – include an analysis of student performance and/or reactions to new practices,	• The portfolio reveals clear evidence of thoughtfulness and reflectivity. • The writer's reflections – reveal new insights on course content, application of new concepts, and/or student performance, – include a general assessment of the strengths and areas for improvement, – reveal struggles with course content and application of new concepts, – include general questions.	• The portfolio reveals some evidence of thoughtfulness and reflectivity. • The writer's reflections – are more summaries of what the writer did than the writer's thinking about what was done, – include vague statements of learning and struggles. • The reflections are unsupported by examples. • The writer has set vague and/or broad goals for the future.	• The portfolio reveals very little evidence of thoughtfulness and reflectivity. • The writer's reflections, if included, are summaries of what the writer did. *continues on next page*	

Hendrick Hudson Teacher/Administrator-as-Learner Portfolio Rubric ***CONTINUED***

DIMENSION	EXEMPLARY	DEVELOPED	EMERGING	UNDEVELOPED	NA
DIMENSION **EXEMPLARY** **DEVELOPED** **EMERGING** **UNDEVELOPED** **NA** **CONTEXT** The degree to which the setting for the story is clearly described.	– include a thorough assessment of the professional strengths and areas for improvement, – include a description of the writer's learning process. • The reflections are clearly supported by specific examples from the writer's work. • The writer explicitly evaluates the degree to which goals have been met and has set specific and realistic goals to extend learning. • The writer identifies specific areas where response is needed.	• The reflections are partially supported with specific examples from the writer's work. • The writer has set specific and realistic goals to extend learning. • The writer identifies general areas where response is needed.	• The writer asks for a response to everything or does not ask for a response.		
	• The student/teacher portfolio design is throughly and clearly described. • The description includes – explanation of purpose(s), – the outcomes/standards targeted, – explanation of how the portfolio fits with curriculum/program, – explanation of the roles of teachers, students, and others in its development and use, – explanation of how the portfolio is managed in the classroom/program, – explanation of how students/teachers select and reflect upon their work, – explanation of how the portfolio is evaluated. • Student/teacher handouts and reflection prompts are included and support the description. • Annotated samples of student/teacher portfolios serve to enhance the description.	• The student /teacher portfolio design is clearly described. • The description includes – explanation of purpose(s), – explanation of how the portfolio fits with curriculum/program, – explanation of how the portfolio is managed in the classroom/program, – explanation of how students select and reflect upon their work. • Student/teacher handouts and reflection prompts are included and support the description. • Samples of student/teacher work from their portfolios are included and improve the description.	• The student/teacher portfolio design is partially described. • The description includes – a list of what students will include in their portfolios, – an explanation of how often and when students select pieces for their portfolios. • Student/teacher handouts and reflection prompts are included.	• The student/teacher portfolio is mentioned, but not described.	

DIMENSION	EXEMPLARY	DEVELOPED	EMERGING	UNDEVELOPED	NA
REFLECTIONS The degree to which the main character, themes, and conflicts of the story are developed.	• The descriptions of the assessments/tasks are detailed and thorough. • The descriptions include – content area focus, – targeted outcomes with indicators, – intended purpose, – detailed explanations of activities that precede the assessment/task, – explanation of how the assessments/tasks fit into the curriculum/program, – explanation of the roles that administrators, teachers, students, parents, and others play in their development and use, – explanation of the amount of time and effort imposed by the assessments. • Student/teacher handouts are included and annotated by the writer. • Checklists and/or rubrics for the assessment are included and are congruent to the outcomes/standards targeted. • Sample student/teacher work is included, identified as anchor or exemplar, and analyzed.	• The descriptions of the assessments/tasks are detailed. • The descriptions include – content area focus, – targeted outcomes, – intended purpose, – detailed explanations of activities that precede the assessment/task, – explanation of how the assessments/tasks fit into the curriculum/program. • Student/teacher handouts are included but are not annotated. • Checklists and/or rubrics for the assessment are included and are related to the outcomes/standards targeted. • Sample student/teacher work is included.	• The descriptions of the assessments/tasks are incomplete. • The descriptions include – the content area focus, – connection to the curriculum/program. • Student/teacher handouts are included but are not linked to the assessment. • Checklists and/or rubrics for the assessment are included.	• The descriptions of the assessments/tasks are nonexistent. • Student/teacher handouts are only partially included. • Checklists and/or rubrics are included, but the reader cannot assess their quality because the description of the task is not included.	
REFLECTIONS ***continued***	• There is a clear and thorough description of the writer's action research project which includes – an explicit, detailed, and thorough rationale for the project, – a specific description of the action(s) being taken and studied, – specific, researchable questions that include the actions	• There is a clear description of the action research project which includes – an implied rationale for the project, – a specific description of the action(s) being taken and studied, – specific questions that include the actions, but that could be rephrased to better guide the writer	• There is a general description of the action research project. The description – vaguely mentions actions being taken, – includes questions that reveal the researcher's area of interest but that are not explicitly connected to actions being taken,	• The action research project needs to be described further. The description – mentions the general area of focus, – includes questions related to the general area but unconnected to actions being taken. *continues on next page*	

Hendrick Hudson Teacher/Administrator-as-Learner Portfolio Rubric ***CONTINUED***

DIMENSION	EXEMPLARY	DEVELOPED	EMERGING	UNDEVELOPED	NA
ASSESSMENTS: Student/Teacher Portfolio Design The degree to which the events of the story (assessments created and refined) are described.	and that will guide the writer in collection and analysis of data, – a detailed list of data collection techniques that will capture actions taken, circumstances of actions, and results of actions and that are realistic and manageable, – a realistic and manageable timetable for collection, analysis, and write-up of data.	in collection and analysis of data, – a detailed list of data collection techniques that will capture actions taken, circumstances of actions and results of actions that may be unmanageable given the time and resource demands.	– includes mention of monitoring techniques, but no specific detail about what kind of data will be collected, when, or for what purpose.		
	• The presentation and organization of the portfolio enhances and showcases the story of the teacher's/administrator's learning. • All parts of the portfolio bear a clear relationship to one another and to a central purpose. • The portfolio is carefully, meticulously, and attractively assembled. A table of contents, sections with labeled tabs, and page numbers help the reader navigate and respond to the portfolio. • The writing is legible, clear, and free of noticeable grammatical errors.	• The presentation and organization of the portfolio help to tell the story of the teacher's/administrator's learning. • The parts of the portfolio are logically organized and help the reader to see the whole picture. • The portfolio is carefully assembled. A table of contents, sections with labeled tabs, and page numbers help the reader navigate and respond to the portfolio. • The writing is legible, clear, and free of noticeable grammatical errors.	• The organization of the portfolio provides some support for the story of the teacher's/administrator's learning. • Different organization of the pieces would make the story clearer to the reader. • The portfolio is assembled in unlabeled sections. There is no table of contents or pagination to help the reader navigate and respond. • The writing is legible. However, the reader struggles with some imprecise language and notices grammatical errors.	• The organization of the portfolio takes away from the story of the teacher's/administrator's learning. • The reader is unable to see the connections between the parts of the portfolio. • All artifacts are lumped together. There is no table of contents or pagination to help the reader navigate and respond. • The writing is sometimes illegible, unclear, and contains noticeable grammatical errors.	
COMMENTS:					

Appendix 4

Hilton School District CLASSIC Initiative Rubric

Goal #1. Development and Use of Appropriate and Authentic Classroom Assessments[1]				
ATTRIBUTE	4	3	2	1
Embedded in Standards-Based/ Authentic Curriculum	The assessment is derived from curriculum-embedded learning opportunities moving students toward mastery of learner standards that tap the use and integration of knowledge and skills.	The assessment is linked to a curriculum-embedded learning opportunity that moves students toward mastery of learner standards that tap the use of both knowledge and skills.	The assessment is appended to the curriculum. It is designed to measure student mastery of learner standards that tap either knowledge or skills.	The assessment is divorced from the curriculum. It requires students to recognize or recall information on topics.
Contextualized and Complete (Reality-based)	The assessment is derived from plausible or real situations that require students to engage with entire problems/situations faced in the real world.	The assessment is derived from a plausible situation that could be real with minor changes. It requires students to engage with problems/situations although not necessarily from beginning to end.	The assessment is derived from one or more plausible elements of a situation that resembles some aspects of reality and requires students to engage with only part of the problem/situation.	The assessment is derived from a situation that is contrived and has little connection with reality. It requires students to solve a part of a problem that is unconnected to a whole.
Integration	The assessment requires students to build upon and apply prior knowledge and skills from two or more naturally related content areas in ways that enhance each area.	The assessment requires students to build upon and apply prior knowledge and skills from two or more content areas that are not ordinarily connected in real life but that support the assessment activity.	The assessment asks students to build upon prior knowledge using two or more content areas that detract from the assessment's original purpose.	The assessment measures students' ability to use a specific skill in a specific content area.
Audience and Purpose	The assessment asks students to work for a real audience and purpose so that they can experience the benefits and consequences of their work.	The assessment has a real purpose and could have real consequences for students if it had a real audience for the work presented.	The purpose of the assessment is vague or only school-related. There are no real consequences beyond the classroom. The audience consists of teachers, peers, and/or parents.	The teacher is the only audience, and the purpose of the assessment is to measure/test. There are no consequences beyond getting credit or a grade.
Disciplined Inquiry	The assessment demands that students search for in-depth understanding through systematic research and inquiry using a variety of sources (i.e., primary and secondary references) and research strategies (i.e., oral interviews, surveys, computer searches).	The assessment demands that students search for in-depth understanding through research and inquiry. Research draws on selected sources and relies on limited strategies.	The assessment demands some investigation or research by the student, but mostly of the nature of finding out facts.	The assessment demands no investigation or research on the part of the student.

continues on next page

Hilton School District CLASSIC Initiative Rubric ***CONTINUED***

Goal #1. Development and Use of Appropriate and Authentic Classroom Assessments[1]

ATTRIBUTE	4	3	2	1
Explicit Standards and Scoring Criteria	The standards of performance for the assessment tasks are clear to everyone. They were jointly identified and articulated by teacher and students who jointly developed rubrics. These rubrics effectively distinguish among levels of performance and guide students in evaluating their work and setting goals for improvement. They are supported with a variety of exemplars and anchors that show students what various levels of performance look like.	The standards of performance for the assessment tasks are clear to everyone. The teacher identified and articulated them in rubrics or scoring criteria. The descriptions effectively distinguish among levels of performance. Assessment criteria guide students in evaluating their work but are not specific enough to help them set goals for improvement. There is a variety of exemplars that show students what quality work looks like.	The standards of performance for the assessment have been partially identified for the students. The descriptions identify criteria but do not distinguish among levels of performance. There are one or two exemplars that show students what quality work looks like.	The student doesn't know what the performance standards are and does not have models that show what quality work looks like.
Communication	The assessment requires a level of communication that is detailed and elaborates on knowledge gained. Communication reflects the learning process through the use of written activities, oral performances, exhibitions, and/or opportunities for students to teach.	The assessment requires communication of knowledge acquired by the student through written, artistic, and/or oral performances.	The assessment requires limited verbal/written communication, limited to short answers by the student.	The assessment requires minimal response from students limited to the identification of answers to multiple-choice or true-false questions.
Meaning to Students	The assessment allows students to feel that the task is worthy of their time and effort and sensitive to their individual and cultural needs.	Students can infer with teacher explanation the meaningfulness of the assessment. The assessment attends to student diversity in very general terms.	The assessment is peripheral to students' lives and does not make reference to the diversity of students' needs and cultures.	The assessment is unrelated to most students' lives, interests, needs, and cultural backgrounds.
Involve Metacognition/ Reflection	The assessment includes measures that guide student self-assessment and reflection on both products and processes. These may include ongoing specific questions, checklists, or rubrics.	The assessment includes measures that guide student self-assessment and reflection on the final product, which may take the form of specific questions, checklists, or rubrics.	The assessment includes measures that ask students to reflect in general on their learning, but questions, checklists, or rubrics are only peripherally related to the assessment.	The teacher is the only person who reflects on the products and process of the performance.

ATTRIBUTE	4	3	2	1
Individual and Group Work	Students work individually and interact with peers to design, implement, and evaluate their projects and performances.	Students work individually but interact with peers to share and give feedback on one another's work during some phases of the projects or performances.	Students interact with peers to evaluate their products.	Students work individually in the design, implementation, and evaluation of their work.
Flexibility	The assessment is flexible in that it allows for student choice of content or of strategies for producing the work and/or demonstrating achievement. Time allotment is also flexible to allow for individual differences.	The assessment allows students limited choice of content or strategies for producing the work and/or demonstrating achievement. Time allotment is somewhat elastic but not necessarily tied to the actual assessment demands.	The assessment allows students limited choice of content (they must choose from a list of topics) and requires a predefined mode of representation. Time allotment is fixed for all students.	All students must work with the same material using the same strategies in a fixed time period.
Ongoing Feedback and Revision	The assessment includes measures that provide elaborate and specific feedback throughout the process from both the teacher and peers. It includes measures that encourage all students to revise in order to produce quality work.	The assessment includes measures that provide specific feedback throughout from the teacher. It includes measures that encourage students to revise.	The assessment includes measures that provide specific feedback from the teacher after the assignment is completed. Revision is allowed but not encouraged.	Feedback on student performance is very general or ambiguous and given after the assessment is completed.

[1] Adapted from Rubric for Appropriate and Authentic Assessment, Learner-Centered Initiatives, 1997.

Hilton School District CLASSIC Initiative Rubric ***CONTINUED***

Goal #2. Emphasis on Reflective Thinking[2]				
DIMENSION	4	3	2	1
Writing and Presentation	Writer's voice is evident throughout. Thoughts are well organized. The writing is focused throughout the reflective piece. Writer supports analysis of questions, problems, concerns with theories, comparisons, conclusions, metaphors, analogies, and clearly linked examples to elaborate on ideas and enhance meaning. The writing evokes thoughts and emotions by the reader.	Writer's voice is evident in different parts of the material. Thoughts are organized and logically presented. Some portions of the material are more developed and focused than others. Writer supports selected part of material with questions, problems, concerns, theories, comparisons, conclusions, examples, metaphors, and analogies.	Writer's voice is not easy to discern. Thoughts are either too general, random, or are not presented in a manner that can easily be followed. The material presented is scattered with many gaps and poor transitions. Writer presents questions and descriptions in general terms with few or unconnected supporting examples, analogies, or comparisons.	Writer's voice cannot be discerned either because the communication lacks focus or development, or because the use of jargon is excessive. Thoughts are presented in very general or incomplete terms. There are obvious gaps and needs for additional information in the forms of examples, questions, comparisons, analogies, and specific concerns.
Self-Awareness/ Process	Clearly identifies and illustrates personal strengths, weaknesses, confusions, and areas of inquiry by specifically stating areas and reasons for their occurrence. Provides insightful information about related and/or future situations.	Identifies personal strengths, weaknesses, confusions, and areas of inquiry by stating areas in which they occur, although does not clearly explain why. Can identify and evaluate experiences but does not differentiate resolved from unresolved issues or questions.	Identifies general strengths, weaknesses, and confusions but does not cite specific examples. Conclusions are vague. Reflection does not include new questions or issues.	Reflects vaguely on strengths, weaknesses, or confusions. Concluding statements are missing.
Risk-Taking (Insightful communication of positive and negative learning experiences)	Honestly communicates positive and negative learning experiences with concrete examples; provides illustrations of learning processes and expectations; effectively defines and clarifies values, thoughts, and feelings about self, students, and/or nature of work. Clearly demonstrates a willingness to change and learn, even to the point of operating differently than the perceived norm.	Communicates positive and negative learning experiences openly but in general terms. Describes learning processes, expectations, values, thoughts, and feelings about self, students, and work conditions. Willingness to change and learn can be inferred but implementation is limited.	Refers to positive and negative learning experiences in broad and unsubstantiated terms. Learning processes, expectations, thoughts, and feelings about work, self, and students are only partially addressed. Willingness to change or learn cannot be determined from information presented.	References to positive and negative learning experiences, thoughts, feelings, or processes about work, self, or students are missing or too ambiguous to be understood. Reflection does not include information that suggests a willingness by the writer to learn or change in any way.
Goal-Directedness	Goals for curriculum, instruction, and/or assessment practice are specific and derived from a thorough analysis of current performance. Suggestions for self-improvement are clearly linked to a review of the strengths and weaknesses of current work. Proposed goals are ambitious but attainable.	Goals for curriculum, instruction, and/or assessment practice are specific and are linked to current practice. Suggestions for self-improvement are generally related to perceived strengths and weaknesses. Proposed goals are not realistic.	Goals for curriculum, instruction, and/or assessment practice are general and/or unrelated to analysis of current practice. Suggestions for self-improvement and proposed goals are too general or too tentative, and are divorced from stated strengths and weaknesses.	The relationship between perceived goals and current practice cannot be established, either because the analysis is too superficial or has not been completely carried out. Goals are not stated in attainable terms.

[2]Adapted from rubric developed by the Long Island Performance Assessment Project, 1997.

Goal #3. Development and Use of Integrated Curriculum and Assessments[3]

DIMENSION	4	3	2	1
Integration of Subjects/Disciplines	The curriculum requires student to use knowledge and skills that show the integration and connectedness between a variety of naturally related disciplines/subjects.	The curriculum requires student to use knowledge and skills that show the integration or connections among two or more naturally related subject areas.	The curriculum requires student to integrate knowledge and skills from two subject areas that are not naturally related.	The curriculum requires student to use knowledge and skills from single subjects.
Meaningful Connections Between Knowledge and What Is Learned in School	The curriculum and assessment explicitly draws upon students' personal experience to make natural connections with what they learn in school.	The curriculum and assessment requires students to *explain* without elaborating on the connections between their own knowledge and backgrounds and the material learned in school.	The curriculum forces contrived connections between the students' own experiences and the material learned in school.	The curriculum and assessment is presented in ways that prevent students from making meaningful connections between their own experiences and the material presented.
In-Depth Understanding	The curriculum is substantive and enables students to search for in-depth understanding of a concept, theme, issue, or problem.	The curriculum encourages students to formulate their understanding of a concept, theme, or issue.	The curriculum enables students to formulate a surface understanding of a concept, theme, or issue.	The curriculum aids students in recalling a concept, theme, or issue.

[3]Adapted from the Curriculum Unit development rubric developed by Learner-Centered Initiatives, 1997.

Hilton School District CLASSIC Initiative Rubric ***CONTINUED***

Goal #4. Alignment of Curriculum, Instruction, and Assessment with District Standards and New York State Standards				
DIMENSION	4	3	2	1
Embedded in Standards	Assessment- and curriculum-embedded learning opportunities engage students toward mastery of District and State Standards.	Assessment- and curriculum-embedded learning opportunities directly relate to District and State Standards.	Either the assessment or the learning opportunities are related to District and State Standards.	Both the assessment and the learning opportunities are unrelated to District and State Standards.
Authenticity of Alignment	Alignment is clear and explicit for both the assessment- and curriculum-embedded learning opportunities.	Alignment of curriculum and assessment to the District and State Standards is clear and explicit but is not embedded in learning opportunities.	Alignment of curriculum and assessment with District and State Standards can be inferred but is not explicit.	Alignment of curriculum and assessment with District and State Standards is contrived and difficult to determine.

Appendix 5

Teacher/Administrator-as-Learner Portfolio Rubric

An Exemplary Portfolio

Overall: The portfolio is a coherent story of the teacher/administrator as a lifelong, reflective learner engaged in the process of making meaning. When reviewing the portfolio, the reader gets to know the teacher/administrator whose work and achievements are depicted and can clearly understand her learning. The teacher/administrator is clearly aware of her audience and provides sufficient description of the context within which her work/learning has taken place.

Dear Reader Letter, Journal Entries, and Other Reflective Pieces: The portfolio provides substantial evidence of thoughtfulness and reflectivity. (For teachers, for example, the reflections reveal new insights and questions related to course content—alternative assessments, authenticity, learning theory, student reflection, rubric development, action research—to the application of new concepts to her teaching and assessment practices, and to student reactions to new practices.) The reflections include an assessment of the teacher's/administrator's strengths and areas for improvement as well as a description of her learning process. The teacher/administrator explicitly evaluates the degree to which she has met assessment goals and has set specific and realistic goals to extend her learning. She identifies specific areas where response is needed.

A Developed Portfolio

Overall: The portfolio is a story of a teacher/administrator as a reflective learner engaged in the process of making meaning. When reviewing the portfolio the reader begins to get to know the teacher/administrator whose work and achievements are depicted and can see that significant learning has taken place. The teacher/administrator writes more for himself than for the audience; therefore, the context of the learning is sometimes unclear to the reader.

Dear Reader Letter, Journal Entries, and Other Reflective Pieces: The portfolio provides clear evidence of thoughtfulness and reflectivity. (For example, for teachers, the reflections reveal new insights and questions related to course content—alternative assessments, authenticity, learning theory, student reflection, rubrics, action research—to the application of new concepts to their own teaching and assessment practices, and to student reactions to new practices.) The teacher/administrator has reflected on his strengths and weaknesses and has begun to describe his learning process and to set specific goals for the future.

An Emerging Portfolio

Overall: The portfolio is becoming a story of the teacher/administrator as a reflective learner. When reviewing the portfolio, the reader learns about the person's work and achievements, but sees snapshots rather than an entire story. The reader can see that learning has taken place, but cannot see how.

Dear Reader Letter, Journal Entries, and Other Reflective Pieces: The portfolio reveals some evidence of thoughtfulness and reflectivity. (For example, for teachers, the reflections center around course content—alternative assessments, authenticity, learning theory, student reflection, rubric development, action research—and application to their own teaching practice.) It is clear to the reader where the teacher/administrator is succeeding and where she is struggling, though she hasn't explicitly stated her awareness of the areas. The reader is able to identify areas for specific feedback.

An Undeveloped Portfolio

Overall: The portfolio includes some story elements, but doesn't yet tell a story of the teacher/administrator as a reflective learner. The reader sees the teacher's/administrator's products, but cannot see the process and thinking behind them.

Dear Reader Letter, Journal Entries, and Other Reflective Pieces: There is little evidence of thoughtfulness or reflectivity in the portfolio. The reflective pieces, if included, offer little or no information about what the teacher/administrator does. They also offer little or no view of the person behind the work. The reader is unable to provide feedback because there is so little information about the teacher's/administrator's thinking and learning process.

Appendix 6

Teacher-as-Curriculum-and-Assessment-Developer Portfolio Rubric

An Exemplary Portfolio

Overall: The portfolio tells the story of the teacher whose goal is to make instruction and assessment practices one and the same and centered around significant learning outcomes. The portfolio reveals the teacher's outstanding ability to apply curriculum- and assessment-related concepts and skills to the development of lessons, activities, and assessments that target clearly define outcomes. The teacher has provided all drafts of assessments, allowing the reader to see changes and improvements made to apply design principles and better align curriculum, instruction, and assessment.

Context: The portfolio provides a thorough, clear picture of the teacher's curriculum, including concepts, themes, skills, and assessments. The connections among these elements are obvious and clear. The outcomes around which the curriculum is designed are significant, precisely stated in terms of student learning, and further described with specific and observable indicators.

Assessment Plan (two to three assessments or a student's portfolio): The plan meshes beautifully with the teacher's instruction. The assessments are learning opportunities and vice versa. The descriptions of the assessments are thorough and provide all the needed context, including content area focus, targeted outcomes with indicators, intended purpose, and detailed descriptions of activities that precede and follow the assessments. The reader completely understands how the assessments fit into the curriculum and the roles that teachers, students, parents, and others play in their use. Finally, the amount of time and effort imposed by the assessments is clearly stated.

Portfolio Design: The portfolio design is clearly student-driven and -owned. It has a real purpose and audience and documents student achievement, effort, and growth toward significant and clearly stated outcomes. The reader clearly sees how the portfolio fits into the curriculum and the roles of teachers, students, and others in its development. The teacher clearly describes how students select and reflect upon their work. To evaluate the portfolio, the teacher uses clearly defined and shared performance criteria, which students use in the evaluation process.

Description of Assessments: The assessments are truly authentic. They are curriculum-embedded, substantive, and integrative tasks that require students to build upon prior knowledge, apply knowledge and skills from one or more content areas, express conclusions through elaborate communications, use meta-cognitive strategies, rethink, and revise. The assessments are valued by audiences outside of school, have a real purpose, and are sufficiently flexible to allow all students choice and opportunity for success. They are relevant to students' lives and sensitive to different needs and cultural backgrounds.

The assessments include measures that guide student reflection on both products and processes that may take the form of specific questions, checklists, or rubrics. Reflections and prompts show the teacher's understanding of the need to accommodate the various developmental levels and learning styles. The teacher has included student work with clear explanations about how the assessments work with different students. The teacher has described the degree to which the target students capture the diversity of the classroom, allowing the reader to draw conclusions about the value of the assessment for wide ranges in student ability and knowledge.

Standards of Performance: The standards of performance for the assessment tasks are clear to everyone. Teacher and students jointly identified and articulated them in rubrics, scoring criteria, and/or exemplars. They effectively guide students in evaluating their work and setting goals for improvement. The rubric design perfectly matches the assessment. Students are able to find the targeted skills at every level on the rubric and can use the levels described to build upon their learning and set specific goals. The lower levels outnumber the higher levels, making the rubric an excellent scaffolding and instructional tool. The top level is above the expected standard—even the highest achiever is challenged to improve. In addition, the rubric includes sample evidence for each level, which the students helped to identify and evaluate.

A Developed Portfolio

Overall: The portfolio tells the story of the teacher as an assessor whose goal is to align explicit instruction and assessment practices, and embed them in a curriculum designed around outcomes. The portfolio reveals the teacher's ability to apply curriculum- and assessment-related concepts and skills to the development of lessons, activities, and assessments that target clearly defined outcomes. The teacher has provided drafts of assessments, allowing the reader to see changes and improvements he has made in an effort to apply design principles and align curriculum, instruction, and assessment.

Context: The portfolio provides a clear picture of the teacher's curriculum. The reader can see the concepts, themes, skills, and assessments that make up the curriculum. The connections among these elements are clear to the reader. The outcomes around which the curriculum is designed are important, are stated in terms of student learning and are further described with specific and observable indicators.

Assessment Plan (two to three new assessments or student's portfolio): The teacher's assessment plan is congruent with his instruction. Many of the assessments are embedded into the curriculum and support learning. The descriptions of the assessments include an explanation of the context, including the content area focus, the outcomes targeted, the identification of the indicators that support the outcomes, and the intended purpose of the assessments. The reader is able to see how the assessments fit into the curriculum and the roles that teachers, students, parents, and others play in their use. Finally, the reader can estimate the amount of time and effort imposed by the assessment.

Portfolio Design: The portfolio design is both teacher- and student-driven, with both parties sharing ownership. It documents student achievement, effort, and growth toward significant and clearly stated outcomes. The reader clearly sees how the portfolio fits into the curriculum and the roles that teacher and students play in its development. The teacher has described the selection process and includes student guidelines for selection and reflection. The reader is unsure of how the portfolio is evaluated or how it relates to the report card.

Description of Assessments: The assessments described include authentic and performance assessments. These curriculum-embedded, substantive, and integrative tasks require students to build upon prior knowledge, apply knowledge and skills from one or more content areas, express conclusions through communications, and use meta-cognitive strategies. The assessments could be improved by providing an audience outside of school, or providing a real purpose. The assessments allow some flexibility in terms of time and measures to allow students some choice and opportunity for success. They are relevant to students' lives and sensitive to different needs and cultural backgrounds.

The assessments include measures that guide student reflection and self-assessment of either products or processes that may take the form of specific questions, checklists, or rubrics. The teacher has included sample student work resulting from the assessment.

Standards of Performance: The standards of performance for the assessment tasks are clear to everyone. The teacher identified and articulated them with some student participation. The rubric design fits the assessment, and the targeted skills appear at all levels on the rubric. The descriptions effectively distinguish among levels of performance. Students can use the levels described to build upon their learning and set specific goals. The rubric may need one or more of the following: (1) more lower levels, (2) a top level that is above the expected standard so that even the highest achiever is challenged to improve, and (3) sample evidence for each level.

An Emerging Portfolio

Overall: The portfolio tells the story of the teacher as an assessor whose goal is to align her instruction and assessment practices and embed them in a curriculum designed around important outcomes for students rather than content objectives. The portfolio clearly reveals the teacher's ability to apply some curriculum- and assessment-related concepts and skills in developing lessons, activities, and assessments.

Context: The portfolio provides a picture of the teacher's curriculum. The reader can see the concepts and themes, but the skills and assessments connected to those concepts and themes aren't as clear. The outcomes around which the teacher is working are important and are, for the most part, stated in terms of student learning. The reader has difficulty seeing the relationship among the outcomes and the teacher's curriculum. The language of the outcomes could be improved by removing references to specific content areas and could be made more clear with specific and observable indicators.

Assessment Plan (two to three new assessments or student's portfolio): The teacher's assessment plan fits in some ways with his instruction. There is evidence that the teacher is aligning assessment and instruction, as some of the assessments are learning opportunities. The content area focus of the assessments is clear to the reader. The reader is unsure of the purpose of the assessment and which outcomes the assessment is intended to target. The reader can see how the assessments fit into the curriculum but is unsure of the roles that teachers, students, parents, and others play in their use.

Portfolio Design: The portfolio design is mostly teacher-driven, and the teacher seems to own more of the portfolio than the student does. The portfolio has a real purpose for the teacher and a limited audience. It documents student achievement toward stated outcomes, but adding documentation of growth and effort will improve it. The reader sees how the portfolio fits into the curriculum, but the role that the student plays in the selection of pieces and the development of the portfolio is limited or unclear. The reader is unsure of how the portfolio is evaluated or how it contributes to the report card.

Description of Assessments: The assessments described are related to the curriculum. It is difficult to determine their substantiveness and rigor. They require that students build upon prior knowledge and apply knowledge and skills from one or two content areas. The assessments could be improved by doing one or more of the following: (1) integrating other content areas, (2) requiring students to do more elaborate communicating, (3) requiring students to use meta-cognitive strategies, (4) providing an audience outside of school, or (5) providing a real purpose. The assessments require a predefined mode of representation and time flexibility but could be improved by providing alternatives for students to choose from.

The assessments may be accompanied by reflective questions that are peripherally related to the assessments. The teacher has included student work derived from the assessments, but information is missing about how these relate to one another. The reader needs more information about the students in order to make any inferences about the degree to which they capture the diversity of the classroom or to draw any conclusions about the value of the assessment for wide ranges in student ability and knowledge.

Standards of Performance: The teacher and students have partially identified the standards of performance in checklists or scoring rubrics, which help students evaluate their work as a whole. While the targeted skills appear at most levels on the rubric, the descriptions have only begun to distinguish between levels of performance. The students can use the levels described to identify where they are on the rubric, but may need more information to use the rubric as a scaffolding tool to build upon their learning and set specific goals. The rubric may be improved by doing several of the following: (1) further describing the levels to distinguish them from one another, (2) incorporating more lower levels, (3) making the top level above the expected standard so that even the highest achiever is challenged to improve, and (4) including sample evidence for each level.

An Undeveloped Portfolio

Overall: The portfolio provides little or no view of the teacher as an assessor working toward integrating curriculum, instruction, and assessment. The portfolio reveals the teacher's ability to teach to the curriculum and to develop lessons and activities. The teacher's assessments are summative only and are designed to measure learning.

Context: The portfolio provides a picture of the teacher's curriculum. The reader is able to see the concepts and themes that make up the curriculum, but not the skills and assessments connected to those concepts and themes. The outcomes around which the teacher is working are curriculum-centered rather than student-centered or are not stated. The reader is unable to tell what the teacher wants her student to know or be able to do outside of specific content-related objectives.

Assessment Plan (two to three new assessments or student's portfolio): The teacher's assessment plan is separate from her instruction. There is little or no evidence that the teacher is aligning assessment and instruction, as most assessments come after lessons and activities and are summative. The content area focus and purpose of the assessments are unclear.

Portfolio Design: The portfolio design is not clear to the reader. The student role is not defined, or the student has little or no role in the selection of pieces for the portfolio. The purpose of the portfolio is unclear as is the intended audience. It seems to be a random collection of student work: the reader is unclear about the intent of the portfolio and how it fits into the classroom or is used by the teacher and students.

Description of Assessments: The assessments described are curriculum-embedded and require that students recall or recognize concepts. The assessments appear to have little relevance to students' lives.

The assessments allow for little or no student reflection. The teacher is the only one who evaluates and assesses the student work. Finally, the reader is unable to see how the assessments work with students because the teacher has not included sample student work.

Standards of Performance: The standards of performance for the assessment tasks are not evident or have been partially articulated by the teacher. Students are unable to use performance criteria to evaluate themselves or improve upon their performance.

Appendix 7

Teacher/Administrator-as-Researcher Portfolio Rubric

An Exemplary Portfolio

Overall: The portfolio tells the story of the teacher/administrator-as-researcher in the process of looking for answers to questions that are at the heart of his thinking. The action research extends naturally from the person's work and drives his thinking. The reader gets a clear picture of a teacher/administrator who is always wearing the "hat" of a researcher—observing, noting, and thinking about what happens and why.

Action Research: The teacher's/administrator's assessment work and reflections clearly connect to his stated research questions. The designed research plan is sound, and methods of collection fit snugly into the writer's assessment design. The research is an integral and natural part of his work. The data collected are clearly presented, accurately summarized, and thoroughly analyzed. The reader can only agree with the conclusions drawn, as the evidence provided is compelling. New questions naturally emerge for the research and provide direction for further study. The teacher/administrator is compelled to continue the quest for answers to these new questions and has clearly defined a plan for continued research efforts.

A Developed Portfolio

Overall: The portfolio tells the story of the teacher/administrator as researcher in the process of looking for answers to specific questions. The writer's research extends naturally from her work. The reader gets a clear picture of a teacher/administrator who often wears the "hat" of a researcher—observing, noting, and thinking about what happens and why.

Action Research: The teacher's/administrator's assessment work and reflections clearly connect to her stated research questions. The research plan is sound and methods of collection fit into the researcher's assessment design. The research is an integral and natural part of her work. She clearly presents the data collected and has begun to draw answers to her questions from it. The reader understands the conclusions drawn and can see evidence in the portfolio to support the conclusions. The teacher/administrator has identified new research questions for further study.

An Emerging Portfolio

Overall: The portfolio begins to tell a story of the teacher/administrator-as-researcher who is looking for answers to specific research questions related to his work. The reader gets a picture of a person who is just learning to wear the "hat" of a researcher—learning to act and think as a researcher.

Action research: The research question is stated, but the reader is not sure how the research connects to the teacher's/administrator's assessment work. The teacher's/administrator's reflections include discussion of the action research, but do not discuss it in light of the other work done. The research work seems to stand apart from his assessment work. The reader can envision how the researcher might incorporate the research more effectively and can see data embedded in the work included in the portfolio. The teacher's/administrator's next steps are to reflect on the research work done and clarify the connections to the assessment work.

An Undeveloped Portfolio

Overall: The portfolio includes mention of action research, but doesn't tell a story of a teacher/administrator-as-researcher. The reader gets a picture of a person who has yet to wear the "hat" of a researcher.

There is no stated research question, or, if there is, the reader can find no evidence that the teacher/administrator is actively doing research connected to the question. The writer's reflections do not mention the research. The reader is unable to see connections between the stated research question and the assessment work included in the portfolio.

Appendix 8

Teacher/Administrator-as-Professional-Developer Portfolio Rubric

An Exemplary Portfolio

Overall: The portfolio tells the story of a teacher/administrator who has clearly defined her areas of expertise and who has outstanding ability to share that expertise. By leading workshops, facilitating collegial circles, coaching peers, and writing articles for publication, the teacher/administrator is contributing to the collective knowledge of other educators.

Description of Activities: The teacher's/administrator's portfolio includes thorough descriptions of professional development activities that build on her expertise. The context is described and consistent with the teacher's/administrator's planned activities. The programs accommodate the various levels of experience of the audience and are based on sound learning theory and an understanding of conditions that support adult learning. The presentation serves as a model for good professional development.

Supporting Resources: The materials used by the teacher/administrator are clear, precise, professional, and attractive. The teacher/administrator has consistently sought feedback from participants and included the feedback in her portfolio.

Reflection and Analysis: The teacher/administrator has reflected on her own learning as a professional developer and specifically discusses strengths and areas for improvement. She has summarized the feedback and has used it to inform future plans. Finally, the teacher/administrator has set clear, specific goals for further professional development activities and documentation of expertise.

A Developed Portfolio

Overall: The portfolio tells the story of a teacher/administrator who has taken on the role as professional developer and is sharing knowledge and experiences with colleagues. By leading workshops, facilitating collegial circles and coaching peers, the teacher/administrator is facilitating the learning of colleagues in his community.

Description of Activities: The teacher's/administrator's professional developer portfolio includes descriptions of activities. The context is described and consistent with the person's plans. The activities accommodate the various levels of experience that the audience brings and incorporate good educational practices.

Supporting Resources: The teacher/administrator uses materials that are clear and neat. The teacher/administrator has sought feedback from participants and has included the feedback in his portfolio.

Reflection and Analysis: The teacher/administrator has reflected on his own learning as professional developer and has identified strengths and areas for improvement.

An Emerging Portfolio

Overall: The portfolio tells the story of a teacher/administrator who has begun to take on the role as professional developer by either leading a workshop, facilitating a collegial circle, or coaching peers. The teacher/administrator is recognized as someone willing to share knowledge and experience.

Description of Activities: The teacher's/administrator's professional developer portfolio includes descriptions of activities.

Supporting Resources: The teacher/administrator uses materials in facilitating the various professonal development activities that are clear and neat.

Reflection and Analysis: The teacher/administrator has reflected on her activities and has identified ways to improve them.

An Undeveloped Portfolio

Overall: The portfolio tells the story of a teacher/administrator who is informally sharing knowledge and experiences with colleagues. The teacher/administrator is becoming recognized in his community as someone who is willing to share knowledge and experience.

Description of Activities: The teacher/administrator briefly mentions his informal sharing activities within the context of his learner portfolio.

Bibliography and Recommended Resources

Airasian, P., & Gullickson, A. (1997). *Teacher self-evaluation tool kit.* Thousand Oaks, CA: Corwin Press, Inc.

Belanoff, P., & Dickson, M. (1991). *Portfolios: Process and product.* Portsmouth, NH: Heinemann.

Bernhardt, V. L. (1994). *The school portfolio: A comprehensive framework for school improvement.* New York: Eye on Education.

Black, L., Daiker, D., Summers, J., & Stygall, G. (1994). *New directions in portfolio assessment.* Portsmouth, NH: Boynton/Cook Publishers.

Burnaford, G., Fischer, J., & Hobsen, D. (1996). *Teachers doing research: Practical possibilities.* Mahwah, NJ: Lawrence Erlbaum Associates.

Collay, M., Dunlap, D., Enloe, W., & Gagnon, G. W. (1998). *Learning circles: Creating conditions for professional development.* Thousand Oaks, CA: Crown Press.

Dantanio, M. (1995). *Collegial coaching: Inquiry into teaching self.* Bloomington, IN: Phi Delta Kappa.

Elliott, J. (1991). *Action research for educational change.* Philadelphia: Open University Press.

Glanz, J. (1998). *Action research: An educational leader's guide to school improvement.* Norwood, MA: Christopher-Gordon Publishers, Inc.

Graves, D. H., & Sunstein, B. S. (1992). *Portfolio portraits.* Portsmouth, NH: Heinemann.

Green, J. E., & Smyoer, S. O. (1996). *The teacher portfolio.* Lancaster, PA: Technomic Publishing Company.

Hewitt, G. A. (1995). *Portfolio primer.* Portsmouth, NH: Heinemann.

Kent, R. (1997). *Room 109.* Portsmouth, NH: Heinemann.

Kimeldorf, M. (1994). *A teacher's guide to creating portfolios for success in school, work, and life.* Minneapolis, MN: Free Spirit Publishing Incorporated.

Lambert, L. (1998). *Building leadership capacity in schools.* Alexandra, VA: Association for Supervision and Curriculum Development (ASCD).

Mandel, G. S., & Smullen, B. C. (1993). *Portfolios and beyond: Collaborative assessment in reading and writing.* Norwood, MA: Christopher-Gordon Publishers, Inc.

Martin-Kniep, G. O., et al. (1998). *Why am I doing this? Purposeful teaching through portfolio assessment.* Portsmouth, NH: Heinemann.

McLaughlin, M., Vogt, M. E., Anderson, J. A., DuMez, J., Peter, M. G., & Hunter, A. (1998). *Portfolio models: Reflections across the teaching profession.* Norwood, MA: Christopher-Gordon Publishers, Inc.

McNiff, J. (1995). *Action research for professional development.* Dorset, United Kingdom: Hyde Publications.

Newkirk, T. (Ed.). (1992). *Workshop 4, by and for teachers: The teacher as researcher.* Portsmouth, NH: Heinemann.

Noffke, S.E., & Stevenson, R. B. (1995). *Educational action research: Becoming practically critical.* New York: Teachers College Press.

Paris, S., & Ayres, L. (1994). Becoming reflective students and teachers with portfolio and authentic assessment. Washington, DC: American Psychological Association.

Porter, C., & Cleland, J. (1995). *The portfolio as a learning strategy.* Portsmouth, NH: Heinemann.

Rényi, J. (1996). *Teachers take charge of their learning: Transforming professional development for student success.* Washington, DC: National Foundation for the Improvement of Education.

Saphier, J., & Gower, R. (1987). *The skillful teacher: Building your teaching skills.* Carlisle, MA: Research for Better Teaching, Inc.

Schon, D. (1983). *The reflective practitioner: How professionals think in action.* New York: Basic Books, Inc.

Index

achievements, in administrator portfolios, 25
acting, teaching compared with, 1
action research, 67
 on adult versus student learning, 74–76
 elements of, 67
 on emotional intelligence, 73–74
 on reading assessment, 71–73
 on scoring rubrics, 69–70
administrator(s)
 artifacts generated by, 5
 as audience for teacher portfolios, 15–16
 job characteristics for, 17
administrator portfolios
 achievements described in, 25
 addressing challenges, demands, and conflicts in, 22–23
 artifacts in, 18
 audiences for, 25–26
 contextual information in, 22
 development of, 17
 goals and strategies in, 24–25
 as learning tools. *See* learner portfolios
 and professional development. *See* professional-developer portfolios
 purposes of, 26
 reasons for developing, 17, 18
 research questions in, 23–24
 as research tools. *See* researcher portfolios
 role description in, 22

Note: **Boldface** page numbers indicate material presented in figures.

artifacts
 administrator, 5, 18–25
 standardization of, limitations of, 6
 teacher, 4–5
art work, as portfolio artifact, 5
assessment(s)
 artifacts, 5
 authentic, action research on, 76–79, **77–78**
 in curriculum-and-assessment-developer portfolios, 46–61
 development of, teachers and, 42. *See also* curriculum-and-assessment-developer portfolios
 good, characteristics of, 46–47, 52–53
 professional portfolios as, 3
 of reading abilities, action research on, 71–73
 in student portfolios, 49–52
 teacher portfolios and, 14
 teacher understanding of, pre- and post-concept map of, **40,** 40–41
 vision for, in administrator portfolio, 20
audiences
 for administrator portfolios, 25–26
 for teacher portfolios, 15–16
authentic assessments, action research on, 76–79, **77–78**

behavioral problems, action research on, 73–74
book project assignment, 53–54
 rating sheet for, **55**
 rubric for, **56**

calendar, in curriculum-and-assessment-developer portfolio, 45–46

Canandaigua School District, New York, principal
  portfolio required by, 25–26
Case, Roland, 9
case studies of students, as portfolio artifact, 5
challenges, addressing in administrator portfolio, 22–23
change, appreciation of, 36–41
CLASSIC (Curriculum Learning Assessment Initiative for
  Children), **11**, 11–12, 95–100
Coalition of Essential Schools, warm and cool feedback
  used by, 82–83
collaborative inquiry, portfolio development in context of, 4
communication, teacher-as-learner portfolios and, 31–35
comparative approach to portfolio, 80
computer-generated presentations, as portfolio artifact, 5
conflicts, addressing in administrator portfolio, 22–23
contexts
  in administrator portfolios, 22
  in curriculum-and-assessment-developer
    portfolios, 43
  for professional portfolios, 3–4
cool feedback, 82–83
curriculum-and-assessment-developer portfolios
  assessments in, 46–61
  benefits of, 66
  contextual information in, 43
  curriculum map in, 46, **47**
  elements of, 43
  exemplary, rubric for, **44**
  learning outcomes/standards in, 45–46
  nature of, 42–43
  rubric for, 103–107
curriculum development
  need for knowledge of, 14
  teachers and, 42
curriculum map, 46, **47**
curriculum units, as portfolio artifact, 4
curriculum, vision for, 20

daily planners, as portfolio artifact, 5
Dear Reader letter, 62, 66
demands, addressing in administrator portfolio, 22–23

educational philosophy, statement of, as portfolio artifact,
  5, 18–22
emotional intelligence, action research on, 73–74

feedback, portfolio, 82–83

goals
  in administrator portfolios, 24–25
  in learner portfolios, 36
  and portfolio framework, 80–81

Hendrick Hudson School District Portfolio Initiative,
  10–11
  guidelines of, 87–90
  learner portfolio rubric of, 91–94
Hilton School District CLASSIC Initiative, **11**, 11–12,
  95–100
Hudson Valley Portfolio Assessment Project (HVPAP),
  8–10, 85–86
HVPAP. *See* Hudson Valley Portfolio Assessment Project

inquiry
  benefits of, 67
  classroom-based, 69–74
  collaborative, portfolio development in context of, 4
  non-classroom-based, 67, 74–79
  and professional portfolios, 79
inservice programs, deficiencies of, 15
instruction, vision for, 20

job description
  in administrator portfolios, 22
  in curriculum-and-assessment-developer
    portfolios, 43
job map, **21**
journals
  photo, as portfolio artifact, 4
  professional portfolios as, 7

leadership philosophy, in administrator portfolio, 19
learner(s)
  versus student, 27
  vision for, in administrator portfolio, 19
learner portfolios, 27–28
  appreciation of change in, 36–41
  awareness of self in, 28–30
  as communication device, 31–35
  exemplary, rubric for, **29**
  goals in, 36
  habitual reflection practice in, 35–36
  Hendrick Hudson Initiative rubric for, 91–94
  prompts for, 39–40
  rubric for, 101–102

learning
- adult versus student, action research on, 74–76
- portfolios as tools for, 81–83. *See also* learner portfolios

learning outcomes/standards, 45–46
learning style inventory, as portfolio artifact, 4
LeMahieu, Paul, 9
letters, as portfolio artifact, 4
looking glass, portfolio as, 3, 13

map(s)
- curriculum, 46, **47**
- organizational, **21**
- of teacher's understanding of assessment, **40,** 40–41

mathematics, problem-solving project in, 48–49, **49**

narratives, professional portfolios as, 7, 88
newsletters to parents, as portfolio artifact, 5
newspaper ad project, 56–57, **59**

organizational frameworks, portfolio, 80–81
organization, vision for, in administrator portfolio, 20, **21**

parents
- letters from, as portfolio artifact, 4
- newsletters to, as portfolio artifact, 5

pedagogy, 14
peer review of portfolios, 9–10, 85–86
peers, as audience for teacher portfolios, 15
photo journal, as portfolio artifact, 4
portfolios
- professional. *See* professional portfolios
- student. *See* student portfolios

portfolio web, **50**
presentations project, 57–61
- outline for, **61**
- rubric for, **60**

principal portfolio, Canandaigua School District and, 25–26
professional-developer portfolios, 68–69
- examples of, 74–79
- rubric for, **69,** 110–111

professional development activities
- for administrators, limitations of, 17
- list of, as portfolio artifact, 4
- problems inherent in, 68
- research on, 67

professional growth, vision for, 20–22
professionalism in teaching, structures precluding, 19–20
professional portfolios
- for administrators. *See* administrator portfolios
- contexts for, 3–4
- development of, 7–12
  - guidelines for, 10
- evaluation of, 5, 6
  - checklist for, 9–10, 85–86
- facilitating use of, 81–83
- forms of, 7
- inquiry and, 79
- as learning tools, 81–83. *See also* learner portfolios
- nature of, 3
- organizational frameworks for, 80–81
- purposes of, distinguishing among, 81
- role of, 2
- structures for, 4–6
  - tight versus loose, 7
- taxonomy of, 7
- for teachers. *See* teacher portfolios

reading abilities, assessment of, action research on, 71–73
reflection(s), 13
- appreciation of change in, 36–41
- awareness of self in, 28–30
- habitual practice of, 35–36
- stimulating, 38–39
- student, 38
  - action research on, 70–71, **71, 72**
  - facilitating, **32, 52**
- teacher, prompts for, 39–40

researcher portfolios, 67
- examples of, 69–74
- rubric for, **68,** 108–109

research questions, in administrator portfolios, 23–24
role description
- in administrator portfolios, 22
- in teacher portfolios, 43

schools of education, limitations of, 1
scoring rubrics
- action research on, 69–70
- as portfolio artifact, 5

simulation, of portfolio development, 4–6
structures, portfolio, 4–6
- tight versus loose, 7

student(s)
versus learner, 27
letters from, as portfolio artifact, 4
reflections of, 38
action research on, 70–71, **71, 72**
stimulating, **32, 52**
student portfolios, 61–66, **63–65**
assessment in, 49–52
development of, 30
guidelines for, **51**
planning sheet for, **31**
project web for, **50**
reflection form for, **32**
reflective questions for, **52**
selections from, **33, 34,** 38

taxonomy, of professional portfolios, 7
teacher(s)
artifacts generated by, 4–5
reflections of, prompts for, 39–40
understanding of assessment, pre- and post-concept map of, **40,** 40–41
vision for, in administrator portfolio, 19–20
teacher portfolios
assessment by, 14
audiences for, 15–16
benefits of, 13–14
content of, 16
and curriculum/assessment development. *See* curriculum-and-assessment-developer portfolios
as learning tools. *See* learner portfolios
and professional development. *See* professional-developer portfolios
as research tools. *See* researcher portfolios
teacher-as-assessor portfolio
checklist for review of, 85–86
teaching
dimensions of, 14
nature of, 1
professionalism in, structures precluding, 19–20
three-part simulation, of portfolio development, 4–6

videotapes of classroom activities, as portfolio artifact, 4
vision statements, in administrator portfolio, 18–22

warm feedback, 82
web, portfolio, **50**
Western hemisphere project, 54–56
reflective questions for, **58**
rubric for, **57**
Wiggins, Grant, 9

About the Author

Giselle O. Martin-Kniep, Ph.D., is the president of Learner-Centered Initiatives, Ltd. (LCI), a research and development organization focused on long-term school- and regional-based curriculum and assessment initiatives. To date, these initiatives include over 3,000 teachers and administrators from over 400 school districts in the United States. All participants in these initiatives have developed and used a professional portfolio as a tool for learning and communication.

Martin-Kniep is also the president of the Center for the Study of Expertise in Teaching and Learning (CSETL), a nonprofit organization that seeks to document and package teacher expertise. The center's activities include publishing exemplary curriculum and assessment materials, as well as planning conferences and leadership programs for exemplary teachers.

Martin-Kniep can be reached at 20 Elm Place, Sea Cliff, NY 11579. Phone: 516-794-4694. E-mail: gmklci@aol.com.